Michael Johnson was born in Yorkshire and graduated
from York College of Art. He worked in a major London
design studio before becoming freelance in 1960, and has
illustrated and designed for publishing and advertising
companies throughout Europe and the USA.

Michael Johnson

PAPER PLANES 2

Grafton

An Imprint of HarperCollins*Publishers*

Grafton
An Imprint of HarperCollins*Publishers*
77–85 Fulham Palace Road,
Hammersmith, London W6 8JB

A Grafton Original 1991

1 3 5 7 9 10 8 6 4 2

A catalogue record for this book
is available from the British Library

ISBN 0 586 21257 4

Set in Stone

Printed in Italy by
Stige Turin

Contents

The author would like to express his thanks to the following:
Aeromodeller magazine for their excellent scale drawings; the Royal Air Force and
Imperial War Museums for services offered by their reference libraries;
Geoff Clark of *Aeromodeller* and Michael Oakey of *Aeroplane Monthly* for their help;
Derek Knight for his advice on electric motors.

The manufacturers of the electric motors mentioned in the text are:
Knight and Pridham, Castle Road, Rowlands Castle, Hampshire.

Introduction

The aeroplanes featured in the original *Paper Planes* were chosen from that early, romantic period in aviation – a period of heroic men and their flying machines – starting with the monoplane designed by the British pioneer Robert Blackburn, first flown in 1911; following this came an early Morane-Saulnier monoplane; two Fokker fighters painted in designs and colours similar to those used by medieval knights for their armour; a very interesting Italian flying boat; the plane flown by the American hero Lindbergh for his epic crossing of the Atlantic in 1926; one of the most beautiful examples of an early 'thirties glider, the German Rhönadler; a small and pretty lightweight Avro monoplane; and finally that classic of biplane design, the Hawker Hart in its polished aluminium and silver finish.

This early period in aviation produced a great variety of fascinating and important designs, which made it difficult to make a selection. In choosing the period from the late 'thirties up to the present day for *Paper Planes 2*, a selection was even more difficult, as design and development have now accelerated to a level where the sheer number of planes produced has reached colossal proportions. Recent technological development has now surpassed designs which not so long ago would have been regarded as science fiction.

Each aircraft featured in *Paper Planes 2* has been chosen for its individual character as well as its significance in the history of aviation. Great care has been taken to keep the selection as varied as possible in terms of design, shape and colour. Finally, of course, their flying characteristics as models had to be taken into consideration, and so their general proportions (wing area compared to flying weight, etc.) decided the final choice.

Large models fly better than small models, generally speaking, so the great feature of *Paper Planes 2* as compared to its predecessor is the size of the finished models. By joining two or even three pages of the press-out parts together, the largest plane, in the shape of the superb Northrop B.2, now has a wing span of about four feet. This aeroplane, along with the Boeing B.52G and the Lockheed U.2R, is in reality powered by jet engines, but from this book these models make up into excellent gliders, looking very realistic in flight.

Paper Planes 2 is after all a book dedicated to the aircraft themselves, their basic designs and, above all, their individual characters, disregarding their primary purpose as war machines. These aircraft have for me, and for many readers, that extraordinary fascination that inspires a highly personalized study of their every detail as flying machines.

The building of all models should be undertaken on a clean, flat table or board. For all scoring, cutting, etc., use a sheet of flat card, or better still a plastic cutting-board.

Before assembling the models, all parts should be carefully pressed out of the die-cut pages, and any rough edges trimmed off with scissors or fine sandpaper if necessary. Make sure that all parts fit together perfectly before glueing in position. Modify if necessary with the knife or sandpaper. In some cases very small or thin parts must be cut by hand, as these cannot be accurately cut by the die-cut process (e.g. windscreens, cockpits, etc.).

In the book we are restricted to one weight of paper, so I suggest in the case of the inside formers for fuselages that these are glued onto thin card or, better still, 1.5 mm or 3 mm ($^{1}/_{16}$" or $^{1}/_{8}$") balsa sheet. This gives a much more rigid fuselage. Reinforcement may be added to the front end of fuselages by way of balsa wood or even solid epoxy (for spinners, etc.). Tail ends must be kept as light as possible.

Extra reinforcement around the inside edges of wing mountings can be made by glueing in a double thickness of scrap paper. This forms a good solid joint when the wings are glued in place.

This double skin technique may also be used in other areas, such as in fuselages fore and aft of the wing mounts (fig. 4, A).

On the Northrop B.2 it is useful to glue an extra thickness of paper inside the wings at their central joint in the area shown in fig. 4, B.

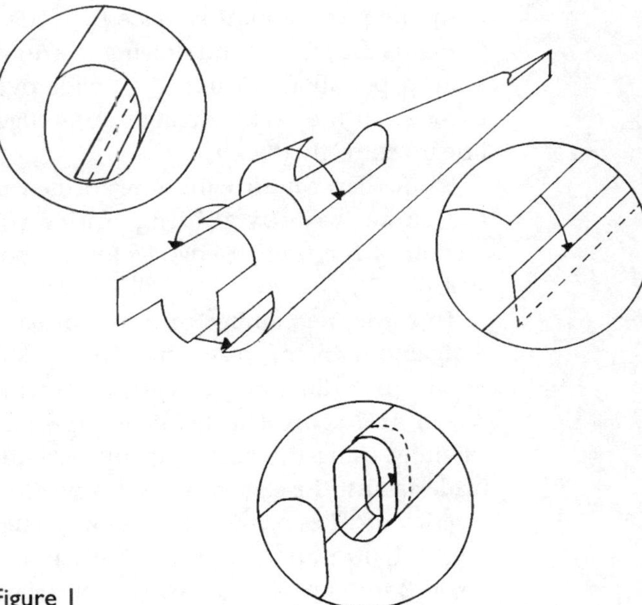

Figure I

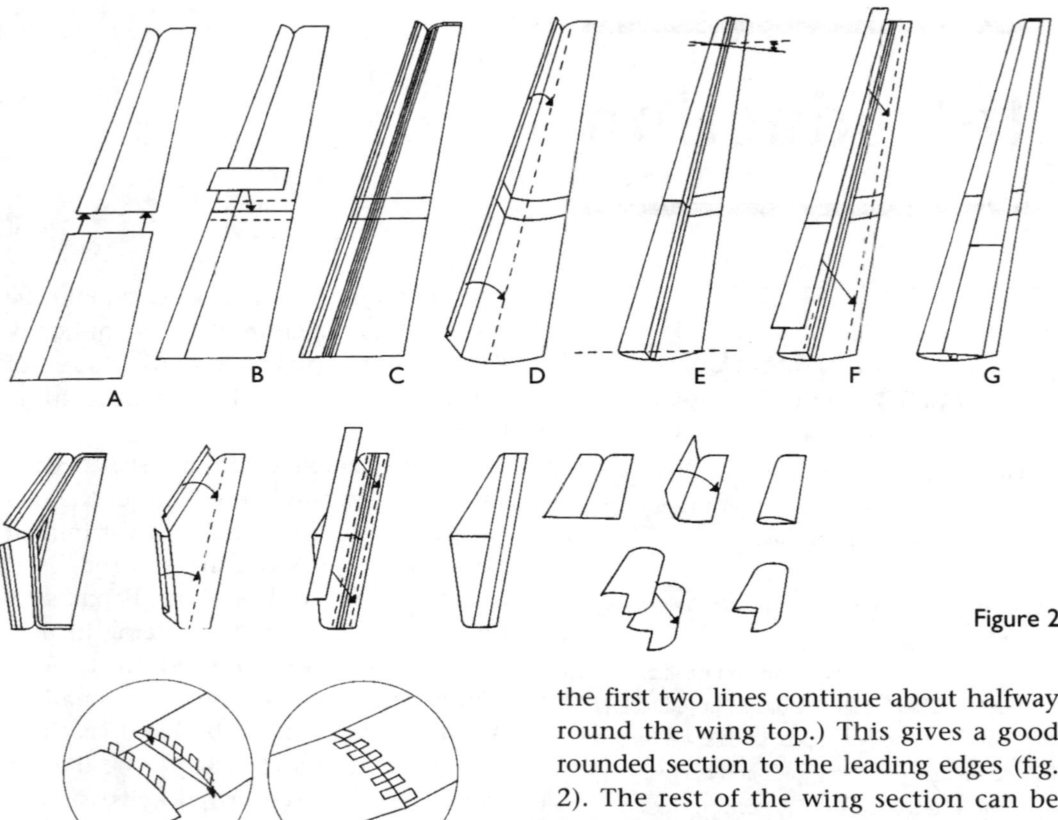

Figure 2

In cases where fuselages are in several sections, joints are made by glueing scrap paper strips on the inside edge, protruding slightly, and plugging on the next section, making sure that everything is in line (fig. 1).

I personally find it best to fit all inside formers *after* each section of fuselage is glued together by sliding them into place on the end of a knife blade or something similar. In this way it is easier to get the fuselage absolutely straight and twist-free. The expert modellers among you may have your own particular construction techniques; by all means use any method you find to be the most convenient.

WINGS AND TAILPLANES (FIG. 2)

On models where wing panels are in more than one piece, a joint is made by placing the parts face-down and glueing a strip of scrap paper about 15 mm ($^3/_4$") wide over the joint at the back, making sure all edges line up correctly (fig. 2).

From then on all wings are formed in the same way: by folding under the section of the leading edge to form a box spar (fig. 2).

To form the camber or curve of each wing and tailplane, place the wing upside-down on a flat piece of card or cutting board and score the leading edge line carefully using the back edge of the knife blade against the edge of a ruler. Now score a series of lines around the leading edge about 1 mm apart at the wing tip and about 2 mm apart at the wing root. (Have

the first two lines continue about halfway round the wing top.) This gives a good rounded section to the leading edges (fig. 2). The rest of the wing section can be formed by drawing it under the edge of a ruler several times, holding the wing by the trailing edge. Care should be taken here to get as near to perfect a wing section as possible.

Once the top curve is correct the box spar section can be glued in position under the wing. Here a small amount of 'washout' (fig. 2) should be twisted into the wing tips. This helps stability by delaying any stalling tendency in flight. Check the amount for each model in the exploded line drawings.

On all aircraft both wings should match perfectly in section and washout, etc.; any uneven twist will have a damaging effect on flying performance.

When both wings are complete, join together at their centres (fig. 2) with a small amount of dihedral (fig. 3 – check exploded line drawings for details).

ANCILLARY PARTS

Undercarriages and struts are made by folding and glueing the paper parts around cocktail sticks or similar pieces of wood, which should first be sanded to a streamlined oval section. Balsa wood can be used for the inside of wheels; this gives a very solid and uncrushable result.

Windscreens and windows can be made

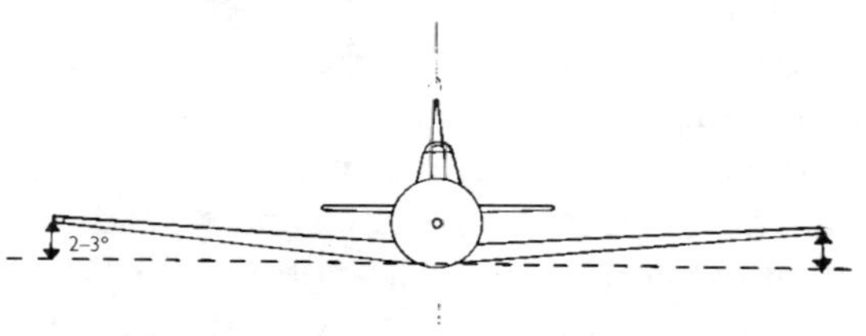

Figure 3

from thin acetate or similar plastic found on supermarket packaging. Another method is to take a roll of transparent self-adhesive tape, roll out a small amount and fold it back on itself with the two adhesive sides together, then cut out the desired shape and glue in place.

Some parts, such as cowlings and wheels, are more rounded than can easily be achieved using only flat sheets of paper. They can be given a more rounded appearance by placing the part on a scrap of balsa sheet or magazine, anything with a slightly soft surface, and then gently embossing from the inside using a smooth, rounded object such as the back of a small spoon, knife handle, paintbrush, pen or similar object. In all cases, when using this technique, make sure that the size of the tool is as close as possible to the curve desired. For example, use a spoon or knife handle for cowlings, a paintbrush handle for cockpit beadings, etc.

If water-proofing of the finished model is required, this can be done by *lightly* spraying with a waterproof lacquer or dope, but check first to see that this does not affect the printing inks. It must be stressed that all spraying must be done sparingly and if necessary using *thinned* water-proofer, as the weight must be kept to a minimum.

TRIMMING AND FLYING

If all instructions have been carefully followed, and the model is assembled with care, the angle of incidence of the main wing will usually be between 2° and 3° to the centre line of the model and the tailplane at 0° (fig. 3). This difference is essential for stability, so check this on each model before making any attempt at flying. Next check that the centre of gravity is in the correct position by glueing a small weight inside the nose – this can be of plasticine, lead or any other small piece of metal.

It is better to *tape* the weight on first, adjusting the amount to bring the centre of gravity into the position indicated in the 'exploded' drawings.

Test-glide until a good glide is obtained and then cut a small 'trap door' under the nose. Now glue the weight firmly in position, after which the 'door' may be glued back into position.

It is now essential to get the model to glide correctly (fig. 5). First test flights can be made indoors if you have a large enough room or hall; if not, choose a calm and dry day outside and test preferably over long grass (for soft landings with no damage).

Holding the model slightly behind the centre of gravity, point the aircraft into the wind (if any) and launch smoothly, with the nose pointing slightly down. This is important; if the model is launched nose-up it will immediately stall. Adjust the glide angle by bending the elevator up or down slightly. For example, if the aircraft stalls, bend the rear half of the tailplane, the elevator, down slightly, and if the plane dives, bend the elevator up. Always make very small adjustments until a perfect glide is achieved.

All the models can be trimmed to glide well, but as all the original aircraft were designed for powered flight, very realistic flights can be made with some of the models by fitting miniature engines.

Because of the size and weight of these models we are restricted to two basic types of motor. The first is powered by CO_2 and can be used with just a few modifications to the airframe, although it can sometimes be temperamental to operate. The charge is made from soda syphon bulbs and great care must be taken when using this motor, as the internal pressure can be as high as 800 psi. The other type of motor is electric and uses rechargeable batteries, driving the propeller via a set of gears. It is recharged by means of a 6-volt dry cell battery (a jack plug is provided). The choice of motor is a question of personal preference. I prefer the electric motor, which is easy to operate and reliable.

An English company, Knight and Pridham, have developed a motor weighing only 26 grams which is perfectly suited to most of these models. Their address appears on page 6. The only modification required is the addition of a propeller to suit the individual aircraft. Take the advice of your model shop or engine manufacturer when selecting a suitable propeller.

Modification of the airframe is also quite simple. First, a bulkhead on which to bolt the engine should be installed. This can be made from very thin plywood or plastic; even thin aluminium, cut from a beer or soft drinks can, would be suitable. Balsa cross-members can be fitted to make the mounting even more solid if required, but take care not to add more weight than is absolutely necessary.

If a motor is fitted, first check that the centre of gravity is in the correct position; if not, adjust accordingly by adding a small amount of ballast front or rear to suit. Then test-glide until a good flat glide is obtained.

The first powered flight should be tried using a short and, if possible, low-revving engine run. When launched into wind, the model should climb slowly, flatten out and, as the engine slows, descend gently to the ground. If the model climbs too

quickly and stalls, pack the engine mounting screws with thin washers to give a little downthrust. If it turns left too sharply, pack the engine mounts to give side thrust in the other direction. If it dives, take off some downthrust.

Flights in large circles are preferable, because the model then lands within easy walking distance. The turning circle can be regulated by bending the back edge of the fin slightly to the right or left as required.

SPECIAL INSTRUCTIONS FOR THE B.2 MODEL

The B.2 is an all-wing or tail-less aeroplane, so requires slightly different trimming. It gets its stability from the 'washout' at the wing tips and the rear edges of the centre section. These replace the effects of a tailplane on a conventional aircraft.

Before construction begins, make up a template out of scrap paper or card to the proportions shown in the exploded line drawings. Use this during construction to make sure the washout on both wings is equal.

For the first test flights *tape* the weight under the nose to bring the centre of gravity into the correct position.

Check again (by looking from the rear with one eye) that both wings are not only straight and true, but also that the washout is *exactly* the same for each wing, and the trailing edges of the centre section (the three points) have a very slight, and equal, upward sweep.

Hold the model by the triangular finger hold, glued under the centre section slightly forward of the centre of gravity. Launch into any wind drift that may be present.

Adjust the glide by means of the two flaps shown on the rear edges of the centre section. Both flaps should be bent up a fraction if the model dives; bent down a fraction if it stalls.

When a good flat glide is obtained glue the weight in position firmly, using the 'trap door' method described in the general instructions.

Fine trimming may now be carried out by bending only the triangular pointed 'tail' located at the rear of the centre section – up a fraction for a slight dive tendency, or down a fraction to cure a slight stall.

Turning left or right can be carried out by very slight adjustments to the two flaps, one having a fraction more up or down than the other.

This model takes slightly longer to trim than a conventional aircraft, but patience will be rewarded with a very good glide.

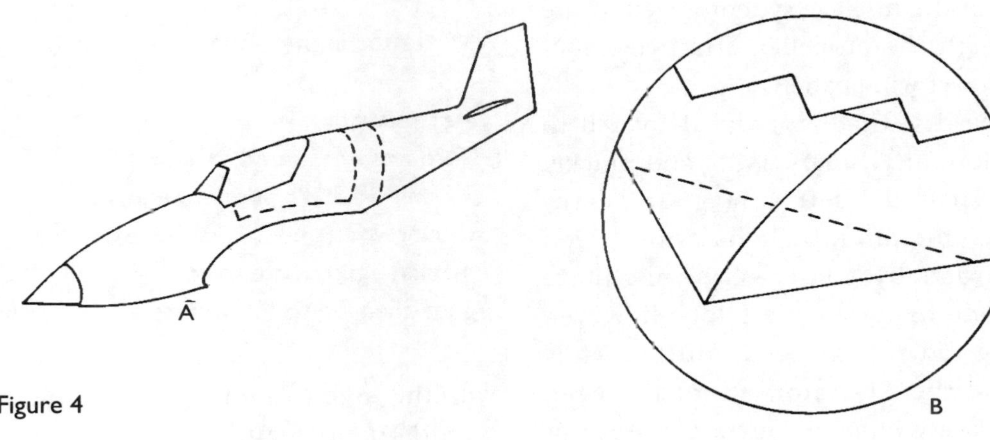

Figure 4

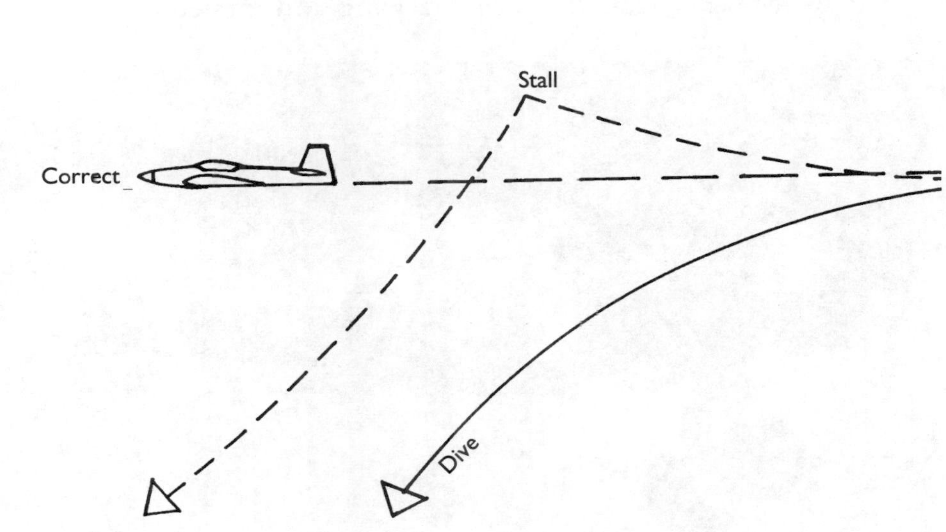

Figure 5

Gloster Gladiator

The Gladiator goes down in history as the last British biplane ever produced. Along with the Fiat CR.42, it marked the end of an era of fighter biplanes which had started twenty years previously with World War I.

It was designed by Henry Folland (whose brilliant capabilities as a designer had been well established for a number of years) as a private venture in 1934. It was in reality a refined development of the Gloster Gauntlet, and first flew in September of that year as the SS.37. It was given the name Gladiator in July of the following year.

The refinements in its design included a completely enclosed cockpit with a sliding hood, single-strut undercarriage, and single bay wings with hydraulically operated flaps. It was later fitted with four Browning machine-guns, two mounted on the side of the fuselage synchronized to fire through the propeller, and two under the lower wing panels.

The first Gladiator was delivered to the RAF in February 1937, and quickly established itself as a good, man-oeuvrable aircraft. It has since been regarded by some as the ultimate biplane fighter. Some pilots, however, preferred the earlier Gauntlet. They found the Gladiator, although faster, not a very forgiving aircraft, and it was thought to be temperamental. If stalled

with the engine running, for example, it would (if not caught quickly) drop a wing and immediately enter a flat spin! (Some old RAF stories tell of pilots landing with wet trousers.)

Unfortunately, the Gladiator was brought into service at a time when the evolution of the monoplane fighter had reached a far greater level of superiority, marking the biplane as obsolete. However, 378 Mark 1s were built, 186 of which were exported to nine different countries. The Admiralty were so attached to it that 270 were ordered for use with the Fleet Air Arm. These became known as Sea Gladiators, and were fitted with deck-arrester hooks and catapult points following naval specifications.

At the outbreak of war, only one squadron remained in southern England to defend the Plymouth dockyards. Four squadrons were already in the Middle East. One of these had become the first Fighter Squadron to be based in Egypt since World War I. Two squadrons were moved to France in November 1939, but unfortunately were no match for the German Messer-schmitt 109s.

The Gladiator squadrons were eventually resupplied with Hurricanes and Spitfires, but one of their last moments of glory came in the battle of Malta in 1940–41, where three aircraft (named Faith, Hope and Charity) earned undying fame in their defence of the island.

LEFT: A Charles Brown photograph of the Gladiator, the last biplane fighter used by the RAF

RIGHT: Gloster Gladiator IIs of No. 33 Squadron based in the Middle East

Hawker Hurricane

In the early 1930s the Hawker Aircraft company's chief designer, Sydney Camm, decided to concentrate his considerable talents on aeroplanes. In August 1933 he discussed his ideas with members of the Air Ministry. Four months later he presented to them his design for a low-wing aeroplane. This was to become the very first prototype for the now classic Hurricane fighter.

This aircraft was in fact a monoplane version of his beautiful Hawker Fury biplane, which in turn had been a development of a series of sleek and successful biplanes which started with the Hawker Hart in 1926. The Hawker company at that time had evolved from the famous Sopwith firm after the First World War, Tom Sopwith himself retaining connections with the company until his death in 1989 at the age of over a hundred.

The Fury monoplane, as it was then known, was built on the Hawker system of a tubular metal construction covered with fabric, which had proved itself in earlier Camm designs. This system was frowned upon by certain designers as

Hawker Hurricane prototype

HAWKER HURRICANE MARK I

Type
Single-seat fighter

Dimensions

Wing span:	12.2 m (40'1")
Wing area:	23.92 square metres (257.2 square feet)
Length:	9.58 m (31'5")
Height:	3.99 m (13'1")

Engine
One 1,030-hp Rolls-Royce Merlin III V12 piston engine

Performance

Maximum speed:	521 kph (324 mph) at 4,877 m (16,000')
Climb rate:	770 m (2,520') per minute
Service ceiling:	10,425 m (34,200')
Maximum range:	684 km (425 miles)

Armament
Eight 7.7-mm (0.303") Browning machine-guns

the trend then was for the development of all-metal monocoque construction. Later the Hurricane was to prove that the older methods were much more practical in wartime. Battle damage could be repaired very easily, and the aeroplane became operational again very quickly indeed.

The original aircraft was designed around the superb Rolls-Royce Merlin engine, itself a development from the engines used in the spectacular Schneider Trophy racing seaplanes. This engine was to become one of the most successful aero engines ever made, later used to power many other aircraft during those war years, including of course that other classic fighter the Spitfire.

The prototype made its first flight at Brooklands in November 1935. Test flights were carried out and the maximum speed was established as 507 kph (315 mph) at 4,938 m (16,200 ft) and a rate of climb of 777 m (2,550 ft) per minute. After these tests, certain modifications were made to the engine, which later became known as the Merlin 3.

The handling was found to be very much to the pilot's liking, being relatively forgiving. Some controls were found to be quite heavy at speed, but the manoeuvrability, particularly at lower altitudes, was excellent.

In June 1936 a production contract was placed with Hawker for 600 aircraft, and by September 1939 the RAF had a total of 18 squadrons of Hurricanes ready for action. Later, during the Battle of Britain, over 1,700 Hurricanes were used in the fighting, over 70 per cent of total victories being claimed by Hurricane pilots.

Further development took place in the shape of the Mark 2C and 2D. Production ended at the end of 1944 with the Mark 4.

The Hurricane was RAF Fighter Command's most important fighter at the time, being used in virtually all battle zones. Apart from the Battle of Britain, it served in France and Norway in 1940, and later in the Middle East, Greece and Crete, as well as in Syria and Iraq. During the North African desert campaign, Mark 2Ds were developed as special anti-tank fighters, being fitted with two 40-mm cannons. In the Far East some Hurricanes were based in Singapore after the Japanese attacked Pearl Harbor. The aircraft was also used by the Indian Air Force and continued its service until the end of the war with Japan in 1945.

Many experimental Hurricanes were built, including a slightly bizarre version with an upper wing that could be jettisoned. It was once towed by a Lancaster Bomber, and was even carried piggy-back on top of a B.24 Liberator.

A unique two-seater trainer, painted bright yellow, was sold to Persia (now Iran) as shown in the photograph.

All told, 14,533 Hurricanes were built.

The paper model is of the silver Mark 1 prototype, which, because of its basic simplicity, shows off the purity of the original design.

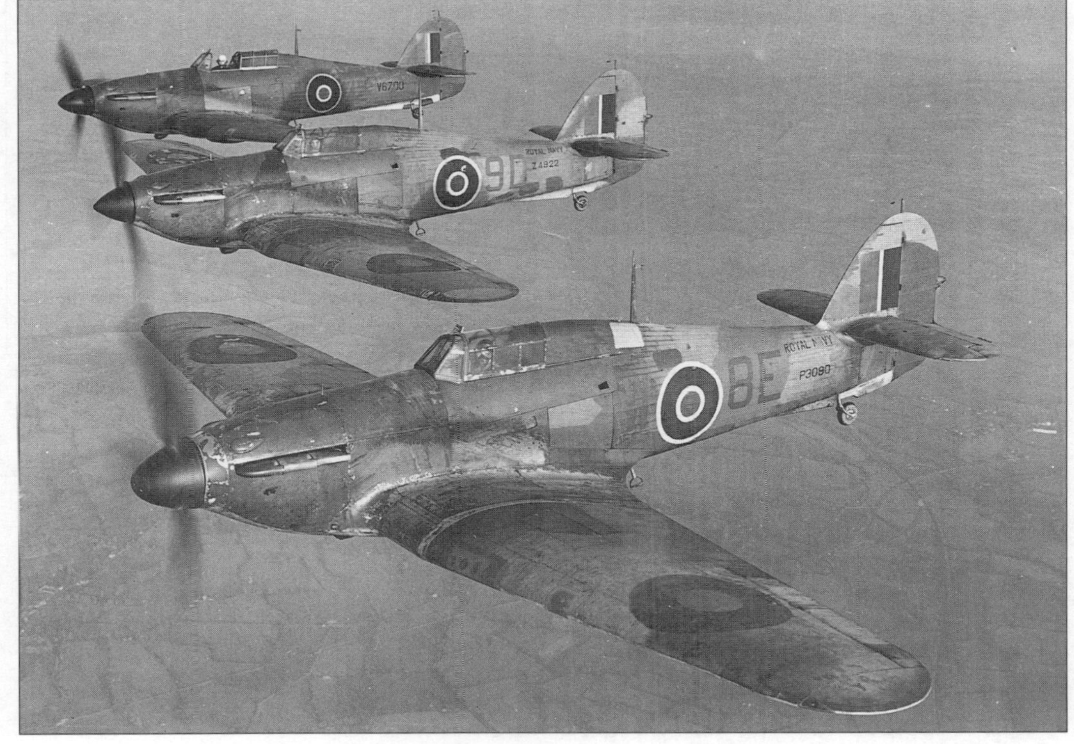

Mitsubishi Zero

In January 1921 a British Air Mission was invited by the Imperial Japanese Navy to advise them on training and equipping their fleet air arm. It was headed by Captain Sir William Francis Semphill of the Royal Navy. This meeting led to the association between Gloster Aircraft and the Japanese armed forces that was to continue into the 1930s.

After long and complicated discussions, Gloster Sparrow Hawk fighters were selected to be flown from the first Japanese aircraft carriers. Fifty of these aircraft were delivered and parts for forty more were assembled later in Japan.

The Japanese aircraft industry at the time depended heavily on foreign designs and designers. The Mitsubishi Company had up to that time been developing engines only, so that when they began their Aircraft Development Plan, one of the first foreign designers to be employed was a Mr Herbert Smith, formerly Chief Designer of the British Sopwith Aircraft Company. This co-operation led to the development of a new carrier-borne fighter identified as the Type 10, which naturally showed certain design influences from earlier Sopwiths.

Along with Mitsubishi, the Nakajinia Aircraft Company was also building Gloster aircraft under licence. These were developments of the Gloster Grebe biplanes, the Gambet, a similar type of aeroplane to the Sparrow Hawk.

In the late 1930s, biplanes were being quickly outdated by the new monoplane designs, so the new generation of Japanese fighters followed this trend in 1937 with the Mitsubishi Type 96 all-metal monoplane, again flown from aircraft carriers.

Development of the 'Zero' fighter began in 1937, stemming from the Japanese Navy's requirements for a new aircraft to replace the Type 96. The spec-

---

MITSUBISHI ZERO
(A6M5C Model 52)

Type
Single-seat fighter

Dimensions

Wing span:	11 m (36')
Wing area:	21.3 square metres (229.2 square feet)
Length:	9.121 m (29'11")

Engine
Nakajima NK IF SAK AE 21 14-cylinder radial, 1,100 hp at 2,850 m (9,350') and 980 hp at 6,000 m (19,685')

Weight

Empty:	1,875 kg (4,136 lb)
Loaded:	2,733 kg (6,025 lb)

Performance

Maximum speed:	613 kph (381 mph) at 6,000 m (19,685')
Cruising:	370 kph (230 mph) at 6,000 m (19,685')
Climb rate:	6,000 m (19,685') in 7 mins 1 sec
Service ceiling:	11,740 m (38,520')
Maximum range:	1,921 km (1,194 miles)

Armament
Three 13.2-mm (0.5") machine-guns, one on upper decking, one on each wing; two 20-mm (0.8") cannons on each wing

---

ifications included maximum speed 500 kph (311 mph) at 4,000 m (13,125 ft), climbing speed 3,000 m (9,840 ft) in nine minutes, endurance $1\frac{1}{2}$ to 2 hours at normal power or 6 to 8 hours at economical cruising speed, provision for two 59-kg (132-lb) bombs, manoeuvrability at least equal to the Type 96 fighter, etc.

The first prototype was completed in March 1939, and in April test pilot Katsugo Shima took the controls for the first flight. He subsequently demonstrated that this was an aeroplane that not only exceeded all requirements, but that it also had the potential of being even more successful than the Navy's most optimistic expectations.

In July 1940 the first batch of these aircraft (the A6M2s) were delivered to the 12th Rengo Kokutai (12th Combined Naval Aircorps) for combat trials in China.

A fascinating design comparison can be made between Japanese development and Gloster aircraft. From the start of their association in the 1920s up until the final development of the 'Zero', the designs of the first Mitsubishi aircraft were decidedly British-influenced. Not only was their chief designer English, but the Japanese air force was in fact largely equipped with Gloster aircraft.

In February 1935, H. P. Folland, Gloster's Chief Designer, started work on a specification for a new aircraft, the F5.34, which developed into one of the best-looking designs for a single-seat fighter of its era. The prototype's first flight was made in 1937. The comparatively slow development was due to Gloster's preoccupation with their production of Gauntlets and Gladiators.

Comparing scale drawings of Folland's F5.34 and the Zero leaves no doubt regarding the very close resemblance of the two aircraft in every aspect. Shape, proportions, wing span and area, engine power, metal-skinned construction methods, etc., plus all the other advanced features of the Gloster, are to be found in the Zero.

This does not diminish the importance of the Zero as the superb aeroplane it was. It only demonstrates similarities of aircraft design throughout the industry at that time, similarities which had always existed and which continue up to the present day.

Modifications to the Zero A6M2s were carried out prior to the start of the war in the Pacific, and on the first day of the war, the Zero spearheaded the attack on the American fleet at Pearl Harbor. From that day it has remained a legend in the eyes of the Japanese, and their former enemies.

TOP: A restored Zero shown here landing at an air show in 1979 (courtesy Frank R. Mormillo)

RIGHT: A captured Zero undergoing flight testing during World War II

Messerschmitt BF.109E

In the early 1930s the German Luftwaffe, which had been clandestinely formed, was organizing competitions to find a new monoplane fighter to replace their ageing biplanes in the build-up to war.

Four aircraft were involved in trials held in Travemünde. Two were high-wing monoplanes, an Arado AR.80 and a Fokker Wolf FW.159. The other two were much more advanced in concept, both being sleek and small low-winged monoplanes. One was the Heinkel 112, a very efficient and well-designed aeroplane; the other was destined to become one of the most effective fighters in the world, the Messerschmitt 109.

Willy Messerschmitt had already been a successful aircraft designer for a number of years, and his experience with his earlier competition gliders and sports aircraft was used to advantage in his concept for the 109.

The concept was brilliant. First he used the smallest possible airframe built around the largest practicable engine. He then pared down the frontal area as much as possible, streamlined the fuselage to its limits, used short, straight, tapered wings, a small fin and rudder, mounting the tailplane low down on the fin, out of the airstream created by the rear end of the fuselage (a technique still used in gliders today). This way he could use a smaller tailplane than usual.

All these points gave the 109 a very low drag ratio, giving excellent handling qualities.

Apart from its basic proportions, the construction methods used were very advanced, incorporating an all-metal, flush-riveted monocoque structure.

The competition at Travemünde was not in fact won outright by the Messerschmitt. A contract for ten prototype aircraft was awarded to both Messerschmitt and Heinkel.

The development of the 109 continued

TOP RIGHT: A 109 bearing British markings undergoing flight evaluation tests

BOTTOM RIGHT: A pair of the later 109Fs

and, fitted with Daimler-Benz 12-cylinder engines, some of the first BF.109Bs were sent to Spain in 1937 to be used by the German Condor Squadron in the Spanish Civil War, where they gained invaluable experience for the later Battle of Britain.

At the outbreak of World War II, Messerschmitt had produced more than 1,500 aircraft, mainly the 109E (named Emil by its pilots), the model featured in this book.

After their Battle of Britain experience, Messerschmitt brought out a new series, the 109F, with a more powerful engine. It was also visually slightly different by way of its rounded nose and wing-tips, improving the aerodynamics and giving more speed.

The 109F was progressively modified with different machine-guns and bomb racks, etc. Eventually the 109G (Gustav) came into service in 1942.

As with the Hurricane, unconventional trials were carried out, such as the mounting of a 109 on top of an unmanned Junkers 88 full of explosives. Another was the use of two fuselages with one outside wing on each, joined together with a stub wing. One pilot controlled it from the port fuselage.

Over 70 variations of the 109 were made and a total of over 35,000 aircraft had been manufactured by the end of the war. No single plane had ever before been produced in such numbers, a record which stands to this day.

FAIREY BARRACUDA

With the build-up of the German armed forces in the late 1930s, the British Air Ministry quickly appreciated the desperate need to build up their own air force, not only in terms of numbers, but also the different types of aircraft that would be required in the case of any hostilities.

Regarding protection of shipping, three types were in regular use. All of these were built by Fairey Aviation and all were outdated biplanes. The Fairey Seafox float-plane was designed for catapult launching from light cruisers. The Fairey Swordfish (nicknamed the String Bag) had already been built in quite large numbers, and continued to be effective throughout the war years. It was used mainly as a torpedo bomber. Last was the Fairey Albacore, which had been designed as a replacement for the Swordfish.

In 1938, foreseeing the necessity of immediately forcing new developments in order to maintain superiority over the potential enemy, the Air Ministry rushed through Specification S.24.37 to inspire a design for a new torpedo bomber. Out of six proposals, two were built as prototypes, one from Supermarine (the Spitfire builders) and the other from Fairey Aviation.

The Supermarine had the unusual feature of variable-incidence wings, chosen by the designer as a means of increasing the angle of descent and reducing landing speed, two important advantages for aircraft carrier operations.

Unfortunately for Supermarine, it was the Fairey prototype that was ultimately chosen to be put into production.

Most of the demands in Specification S.24.37 had been satisfied, although the aircraft had been criticized by some as looking ungainly when on the ground. These reservations had been dismissed, as obviously its performance in the air was more important.

FAIREY BARRACUDA

Type
Torpedo and dive-bomber with crew of three

Dimensions

Wing span:	15 m (49' 2") Marks 1–3,
	16 m (53') Mark 5
Length:	12 m (39' 9") Marks 1–3,
	12.5 m (41' 7") Mark 5,
Height:	4.5 m (15' 2") Marks 1–3,
	5.25 m (17' 3") Mark 5

Engine
Rolls-Royce Merlin 30 of 1,300 hp (Mk 1)
Rolls-Royce Merlin 32 of 1,640 hp (Mk 2)
Rolls-Royce Griffon 8 of 2,020 hp (Mk 5)

Performance

Maximum speed:	378 kph (235 mph) at 3,353 m (11,000') (Mk 1)
	407 kph (253 mph) at 3,353 m (11,000') (Mk 5)
Service ceiling:	5,608 m (18,400') (Mk 1)
	6,096 m (20,000') (Mk 3)
	7,315 m (24,000') (Mk 5)
Range:	2,124 km (1,320 miles) (Mk 1)
	1,802 km (1,120 miles) (Mk 5)

Weight

Empty:	3,946 kg (8,700 lb) (Mk 1)
	4,241 kg (9,350 lb) (Mk 2)
	4,264 kg (9,400 lb) (Mk 3)
	5,185 kg (11,430 lb) (Mk 5)
Loaded:	6,124 kg (13,500 lb) (Mk 1)
	6,396 kg (14,100 lb) (Mk 2)
	6,917 kg (15,250 lb) (Mk 5)

Armament
Two 7.7-mm (0.303") Vickers machine-guns in rear cockpit. One 1,620-lb torpedo or up to 1,800 lb of bombs

This prototype now became known as the Fairey type 100 Barracuda.

Designed by M. J. O. Lobelle, it had a distinctive appearance. Its wings, mounted at shoulder level on the fuselage, had large exterior flaps which, apart from their normal purpose, could also be used as dive brakes. It was powered with a Rolls-Royce 1,300-hp Merlin 30. During its first flight trials on 7 December 1940 trouble was experienced with the tailplane; it was subsequently raised high on the fin, thus curing problems with turbulence.

The second prototype appeared in 1941 and a third, the Mark 2, in 1942. This had the more powerful 1,640-hp Merlin 32 engine driving a four-bladed propeller.

Mark 3 was brought out in 1943, the main difference being the installation of anti-submarine radar equipment. More development continued with the installation of an even more powerful engine, this time the Rolls-Royce Griffon 7 giving 1,850 hp. The final Mark 5 was given even more power with the Griffon 8 giving 2,020 hp. Other modifications included the increase in wing span to just over 16 m (55 ft). The airframe was strengthened and its electrical system modified.

During the war not a great deal of use was made of the Barracuda as a torpedo bomber. It did however prove to be very effective on anti-submarine patrols, and as a dive bomber. The fortunate few who witnessed a whole squadron of Barracudas peeling off one after the other into a dive treasured a spectacle never to be forgotten.

Charles Brown photographs showing Mark IIs
carrying torpedoes and, at right, Mark Is with
radar aerials on the wings

BOEING B.52 SUPERFORTRESS

Towards the end of October 1948, a group of engineers from the Boeing Aircraft Company presented their proposed design for the XB.52 bomber to the US Air Force, only to be informed that the specification had been changed and must now include provision for in-flight refuelling and turbojet engines to give the aircraft a much longer range. This meeting was on a Friday, so the whole team booked into a nearby hotel, sharpened their pencils, and set about redesigning their aircraft, which needed more wing area and sweepback, as well as scope for eight Pratt & Whitney J.57 turbojet engines. After many hours of intensive calculations a new design was produced. The completed drawings were then rushed to a local model-maker who very quickly put together a scale model.

All these elements were presented at the Monday morning meeting with the Air Force representatives who, after careful scrutiny, accepted it and gave the go-ahead for the production of Model 464.67, later to be known as the B.52 – the longest-serving bomber in history. The first flight trials started in April 1952 and it is planned to keep the type operational until the end of this century.

The B.52's development followed the Boeing B.47 Stratojet, another swept-back wing design with six jet engines (influenced by late wartime German development). The B.52 was designed as a much larger long-range bomber, whereas the B.47s were used only for intelligence-gathering. It first saw service with the Strategic Air Command in June 1955, based in California. The late 1950s were rife with fear of nuclear alerts, so the strike potential of the US Air Force had to be publicized by the media in general to calm the nerves of an American nation under threat of Communist attack. Films like *Bombers B.52* and *A Gathering of Eagles*, starring Karl Malden and Rock Hudson respectively, were apparently partly sponsored by the SAC. The atomic bomb was, of course, regarded by the general public as a horrifying weapon, so very little reference was made by Hollywood to the nature of the weapons carried by the aircraft.

Many versions of the B.52 have been produced but it still retains its original shape. The models started with the B.52A, B and C and continued through to G and the latest version, H, which is fitted out to carry the very latest nuclear missiles, as well as all the most recent highly sophisticated radar and electronic equipment.

Over the years, the aircraft came in a variety of colours and finishes –

BOEING B.52 SUPERFORTRESS

Type
Six-seat long-range bomber (nuclear and conventional)

Dimensions

Wing span:	56.39 m (185')
Wing area:	372 square metres (4,000 square feet)
Length:	49.04 m (160'11")
Height:	12.4 m (40' 8")

Engines
Eight Pratt & Whitney T.F. 33 P.3 turbofans, each producing 7,711 kg (17,000 lb) static thrust

Performance

Maximum speed:	958 kph (595 mph) at 36,000'
Range:	16,093 km (10,000 miles)

Weight

Empty:	74,864 kg (165,000 lb)
Maximum at take-off:	221,363 kg (488,000 lb)

Armament

Nuclear:	Eight B43 or twelve B61 missiles
Conventional:	up to 108 MK82 bombs

BELOW LEFT: A B.52 landing, showing the huge wing flaps in the down position

LEFT: A B.52 in flight

BELOW: An early model B.52 being serviced

(all photographs courtesy Aeroplane Monthly)

polished aluminium and silver paint, two-tone silver and white, variegated green camouflaged top surfaces with white underneath, all beige. In its most sinister-looking version it was painted all black with only the upper surfaces camouflaged in dark green. The latest versions are dark grey and green overall. The B.52 has been nicknamed BUFF (big, ugly, fat ... fella is the polite version). Big it certainly is (as can be verified by anyone who has walked under or around it), having a wing span of 56.39 m (185 ft) and a length of 49.04 m (160 ft 11 in).

Ugly? Not for me. I find the simplicity of its design very appealing. Its fuselage is in fact quite slim when compared to its length. Its wings, with their sweepback and well-balanced proportions, combine with the tail surfaces to form all the ingredients of an excellent model glider.

Lockheed U.2R

Francis Gary Powers had taken off from the US airbase near Peshawar in Pakistan in the early morning of 1 May 1960. Climbing steadily, he reached his cruising altitude of over 21,000 m (70,000 ft) and headed north.

'Frank' Powers was flying for the CIA, and his mission that day was to overfly the Russian Intercontinental Ballistic Missile test sites at Sverdlovsk, gathering photographic and other intelligence information. May Day had been chosen in the knowledge that it was a national holiday, and hopefully the early-warning radar stations would be short-staffed. Nevertheless, the aircraft had been located and the alert given, causing intense ground activity.

The unfortunate Powers, now cruising some 22 km (14 miles) overhead, did not see the Mig 19 interceptor take off, nor did he hear the explosions signalling the launch of more than a dozen SA2 'Guideline' missiles.

The shock waves of the intense explosions under and around the aircraft wrecked most of the fuselage, shattered the fin and tailplane, and blew both wings off completely. What was left of the wreck dived like a shot bird and went into a terrifying inverted spin. Powers opted for an attempt to climb out rather than risk injury by ejecting. Amazingly, he managed to bail out relatively unhurt. Floating down on his parachute, he had no idea that within a few days his dramatic story would be in the headlines of every newspaper and television report around the world.

After statements by the CIA and President Eisenhower, denying any flying over the Soviet missile sites, the Russians promptly produced not only Powers himself, but also the cameras and spying equipment recovered from the wreckage. After a much-publicized trial, Powers was convicted of spying

and given a long jail sentence, but after two years in prison he was released in exchange for a KGB agent.

All this added yet another very embarrassing incident to the 'cold' war between Russia and the Western powers. On the other hand, it did bring out into the open the type of aircraft used for this sort of operation; the plane in question was the now infamous Lockheed U.2.

Spy planes, or strategic reconnaissance aircraft as the authorities now prefer to call them, had been used in warfare from the early days of flying. During the 1914–18 war, kites, balloons and 'spotting' planes were used by both sides to check on each other's defence systems. This type of aerial espionage played a major role in the battlefields,

giving the military great advantages over their opponents. By documenting the layout of installations and the troop movements of the enemy, they derived a great deal more flexibility for their own actions.

Just before the Second World War started in 1939, reconnaissance flights were already being made over Germany with a civil-registered Lockheed 12A, with a mission to photograph various military and naval installations, thus providing invaluable information for later bombing raids during the first few months of the war. This type of operation led to the formation of England's first aerial espionage unit, which in 1940 became known as the RAF's Photographic Development Unit. As the war developed, this unit used modified Spitfires and twin-engined de Havilland Mosquitoes for various types of photo-reconnaissance work.

The end of World War II led to a deterioration of relations between Russia and the West, provoking rapid developments in strategic reconnaissance by both sides. High-flying converted bombers, fitted with domes and blisters (to house their intelligence-gathering equipment), were constantly overflying each other's territory in an attempt to keep abreast of all the latest military developments. Clandestine operations of this kind invariably led to the shooting down of many aircraft long before the Gary Powers incident.

It was not long before the American military and the CIA in particular came to an understanding of the need for an aircraft specifically designed for these kinds of spying duties. This led to the drawing up of a specification to be presented to various aircraft manu-facturers. In a short time proposals were offered by the Bell Company and Lockheed.

The Lockheed project, designed by Clarence L. (Kelly) Johnson, was

---

LOCKHEED U.2R

Type
Single-seat reconnaissance aircraft

Dimensions

Wing span:	31.5 m (103'4")
Wing area:	93 square metres (1,001 square feet)
Length:	19.2 m (63'1")
Height:	4.9 m (16'2")
Weight:	13,925 kg (30,700 lb)
Extra payload:	1,792 kg (3,950 lb)

Engine
One Pratt & Whitney J75P13A turbojet giving 7,711 kg (17,000 lb) thrust

Performance

Maximum speed:	862 kph (536 mph) at 10,668 m (35,000')
Cruising speed:	700 kph (435 mph) at 21,946 m (72,000')
Service ceiling:	23,774 m (78,000')
Range:	12,070 km (7,500 miles)
Endurance:	15 hours

A U.2 trailing a parachute, used to slow aircraft down during landing *(courtesy Aeroplane Monthly)*

carefully studied and initially rejected by the Air Force, on the grounds that the recommended engine (the J59) could not be installed. The CIA, however, showed great interest in this project and, after more discussion, Johnson agreed to the modifications required to install the larger engine. He was then given the go-ahead for the building of the first prototype.

Within nine months top-secret flight trials of what became known as 'Kelly's Angel' took place in the Nevada Desert.

The aircraft, later designated the U.2, had the appearance of a large sailplane, with its slim fuselage and long high-aspect-ratio wings, high tail fin and bicycle-style undercarriage. The whole aircraft had been designed with weight saving as a priority, giving it a very light wing loading at the expense of structural strength. This, combined with the fact that it was difficult to fly, led

later to many unfortunate accidents and lost lives.

Steady development of the U.2 programme took place over three decades, both of the airframe itself and of its photographic and electronic equipment. As far back as 1955, autofocus and autoexposure cameras had been developed for photo-reconnaissance. Used with stereo lenses, photographs with incredible definition could be produced. (As proof of this quality, the USAF released pictures showing a golf course where it was possible to make out the golf balls lying in the grass; all this from 6 kilometres (4 miles) high, using negatives 46 cm (18 inches) square.) Other cameras were specifically designed for the U.2s by E. Land, the Polaroid inventor, and astronomer Dr J. Baker, using a 33-cm (13-inch) lens and special lightweight film produced by Kodak. In a single

mission, up to 4,000 photographs could be taken. These were then processed and fitted together in a grid system to give a huge, highly detailed map of the particular region under surveillance.

Design developments over the years changed the proportions and size of the aircraft. The early U.2 A, B, C and D models were shorter in fuselage length and wing spans than the later U.2Rs, which were subsequently refined even further to become the TR1s. These later models, with their excellent endurance and altitude performance, combined with their now even more sophisticated optical and electronic sensors, continue to be as effective today as the early U.2s of over thirty years ago.

NORTHROP B.2 'STEALTH' BOMBER

If ever an aircraft could be described as looking like something out of a science fiction movie, it must surely be the Northrop B.2. With its unmistakable, and quite remarkable, geometric shape, this flying wing is the outcome of one of the most unprecedented design and development programmes ever undertaken, and takes its place as perhaps the most advanced aeroplane in the world today.

Advanced it certainly is, but its costs are even more staggering. A Frenchman recently said, 'It took Pearl Harbor for President Roosevelt to convince the Senate to accept a war. Russian space development forced Kennedy into the Apollo space programme. What can it be that has provoked this massive American reaction materializing in the B.2, costing close to six hundred million dollars each! And they are talking about producing a hundred and thirty-two.'

The dimension of this vast operation is understood better when one realizes that all the large American aviation companies are involved. Boeing, General Dynamics, Lockheed, General Electric, Vaught Hughes, Rockwell, MDD, Honeywell, etc., are all contributing; no one has been omitted. The Northrop company acts as co-ordinator for the whole massive programme.

The B.2 was rolled out of its Palmdale, California, hangar in November 1988 in front of a carefully selected audience who, I am sure, were suitably impressed. Its first flight took place on 17 July of the following year, culminating in an exhaustive test programme at the Edwards Air Base.

The flying-wing form was chosen for several reasons. First (as demonstrated by Alexander Lippitsch and the Horten Brothers in the 1930s) a tail-less or all-wing aircraft, having no tailplane or fins, has much lower drag and is consequently much more efficient aerodynamically. All fuel, cargo or weapons, together with the crew, can be housed in the wing itself, giving it an unrivalled advantage over conventional aircraft. Secondly, the general shape of a flying wing has excellent 'stealth' properties – the swept-back leading edges, the large 'saw tooth' trailing edges, the inlet edges to the engines (again a zig-zag shape) all have radar-scattering capabilities. Combine all this with an external finish in a Radar-Absorbent Material (RAM) and the aircraft becomes almost undetectable.

The entire aircraft was designed on computers, using over 400 machines connected to a database managed by a Cray super-computer. The designers worked from the outside in; when each part was completed, it was fed into the main database. That way every single component's location could be defined down to the most minute detail.

The flight control of the B.2 was given special consideration. Because the centre of gravity is behind the centre of lift, the machine is inherently unstable. The belief is that the commands are carried to the control activators by light signals using fibre-optics – fly by light rather than fly by wire (FBW controls are now used by the most modern aircraft). Fly by light has another, rather 'dark' advantage. It is highly resistant to the electromagnetic pulses caused by nuclear explosions.

Construction methods in the B.2 use many composite materials. Carbon fibre, kevlar and other exotic resin-based plastics are used throughout, making it by far the largest aircraft ever made by these processes. The whole assembly is rather like putting together a giant plastic kit with two half shells, inside which frames and spans form separations for the different compartments, such as the cockpit, engines, bomb bays, fuel tanks, etc. On completion, the aircraft is totally white before the application of the final coating of RAM.

Flying-wing or tail-less aircraft are not new to the Northrop company. Jack Northrop had already produced several different types in the years of the Second World War. From the outset the planes were plagued with problems – marginal stability and unreliable

---

NORTHROP B.2 'STEALTH' BOMBER

(All figures are approximate)

Type
Long-range strategic bomber (nuclear).
Two or three crew

Dimensions

Wing span:	52.43 m (172')
Length:	21.03 m (69')
Height:	5.18 m (17')

Performance

Maximum speed: mach 9, 1,010 kph (628 mph) at 15,240 m (50,000')

Range: 9,655 km (6,000 miles); with one refuelling more than 16,100 km (10,000 miles)

Engines
Four General Electric F118-GE-100 turbofans producing 8,618 kg (19,000 lb) thrust each. No afterburners

Weight

Empty:	54,432 kg (120,000 lb)
Maximum:	158,760 kg (350,000 lb)

Armament
Two internal weapon bays could carry SRAM11 nuclear missiles or B61 or B83 free-fall nuclear bombs or a wide variety of conventional bombs. Total weapon load approximately 22,680 kg (50,000 lb)

engines to name but two. After several accidents and a great deal of expense the whole flying-wing programme was scrapped in 1950.

In fact, the flying-wing concept has been present throughout the history of aviation, with the early pioneer J. W. Dunne producing some very advanced designs in the early 1900s. In Germany, Hugo Junkers took out a patent on what was then called an all-wing design, although this did in fact have a stabilizer. G. T. R. Hill produced a true all-wing aircraft called the Pterodactyl in 1928.

In the 1920s and 1930s two (or actually three) designers stand out for early important and very creative work on the all-wing concept. These were the Germans, Alexander Lippitsch and the two Horten brothers.

Lippitsch started his research in the early 1920s with all-wing gliders, later moving on to develop his delta-wing aircraft, culminating in the rocket-powered Messerschmitt 163 in 1943 – the forerunner of all modern jet-powered aircraft.

The Horten Brothers, Walter and Reimar, must be given credit for being the most influential in the development of all-wing aircraft, from their early, very beautiful sailplanes to their final designs at the end of World War II. For almost thirty years they had concentrated their efforts on the all-wing concept, convinced that this was the ultimate direction for aircraft design. Unfortunately for them, with the ending of the war with Germany, the Allies took over their small factory in Bonn and shipped the remaining aircraft first to England and then on to the USA for detailed study. The H.9 (*circa* 1944) is now in the Smithsonian Institution, where close examination of its proportions, twin jet engine position, general shape, and all-composite construction shows marked similarities to the new Northrop that has appeared more than forty years later.

The B.2 was designed primarily as the main penetration bomber for the USAF Strategic Air Command in the 1990s. It is capable of carrying a load of SRAM nuclear missiles or B83 free-fall nuclear bombs; a wide variety of conventional bombs could replace the nuclear weapons. Its total weapon load could be approximately 22,680 kg (50,000 lb). Combining its high-flying potential and enormous range, it could fly from, say, a Texas air base to anywhere in the world to drop its awesome cargo; this, combined with its highly sophisticated electronic sensors and 'stealth' potential, makes it perhaps the most formidable bomber of all time.

This leads to the question as to whether or not it was used in Iraq, a question that must remain unanswered for the moment. The only speculations we are able to make are to compare its history with other aircraft development programmes. Normally, the time between prototype flight tests and operational availability is in the region of one to one and a half years. The B.2 has been flying for over two years. Using its computerized design programme would cut down the testing time considerably (the computer is able to give answers to flight and operational questions long before the aircraft has even left the ground). Iraq could therefore have made a perfect test range.

This photograph of the B.2 taken during flight testing shows to advantage its remarkable plan form *(photograph via Aeroplane Monthly)*

GLOSTER GLADIATOR

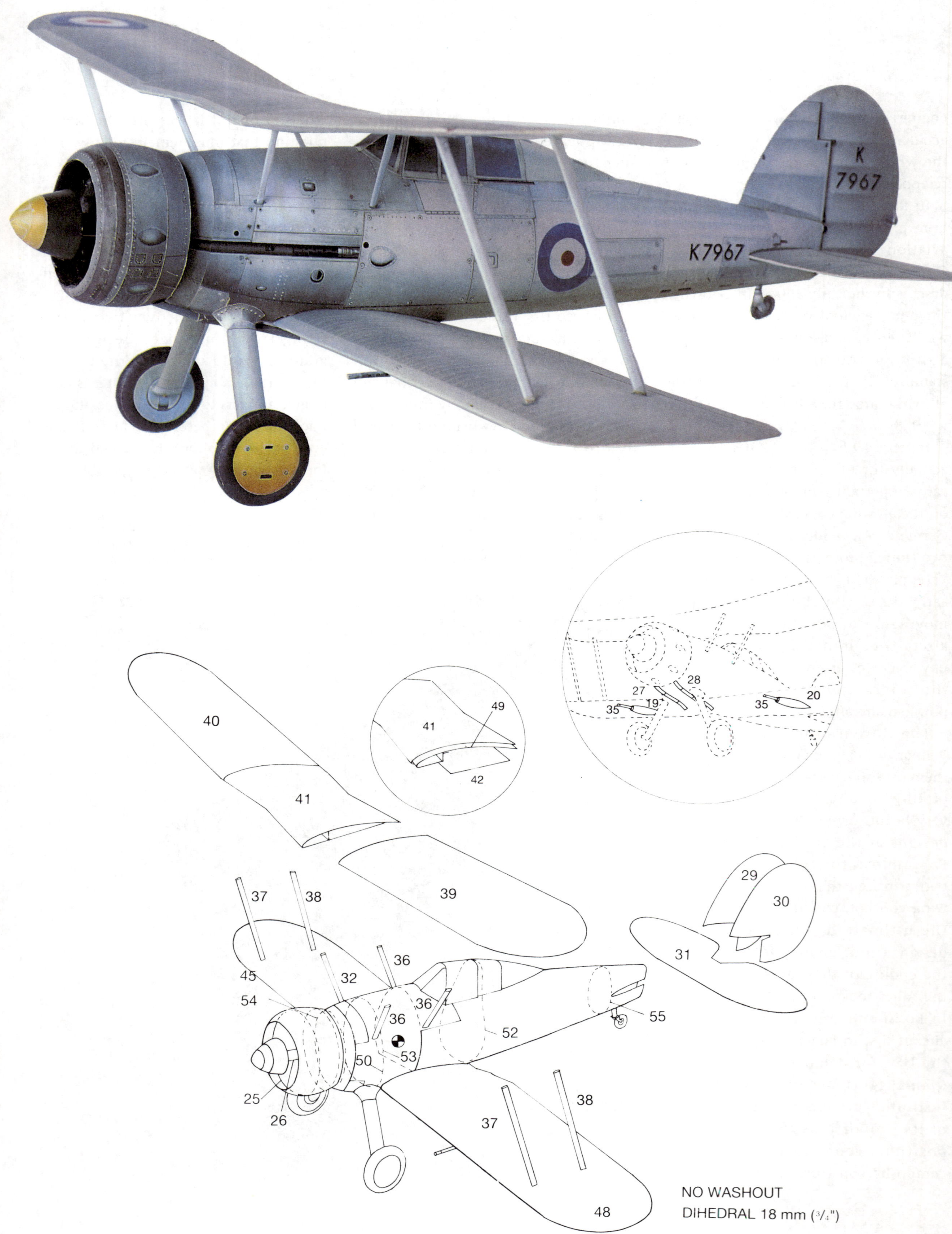

GLOSTER GLADIATOR

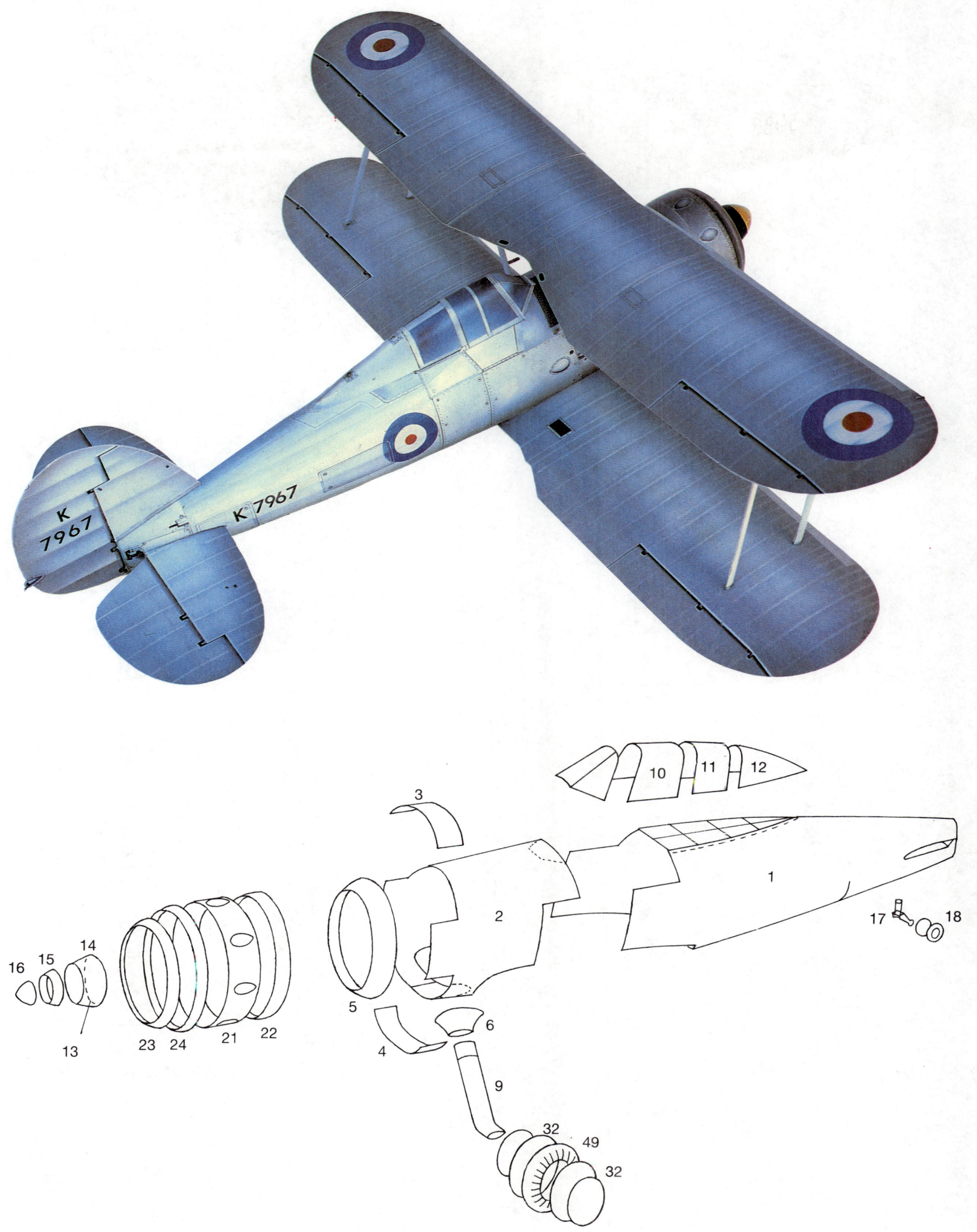

HAWKER HURRICANE

HAWKER HURRICANE

MITSUBISHI ZERO

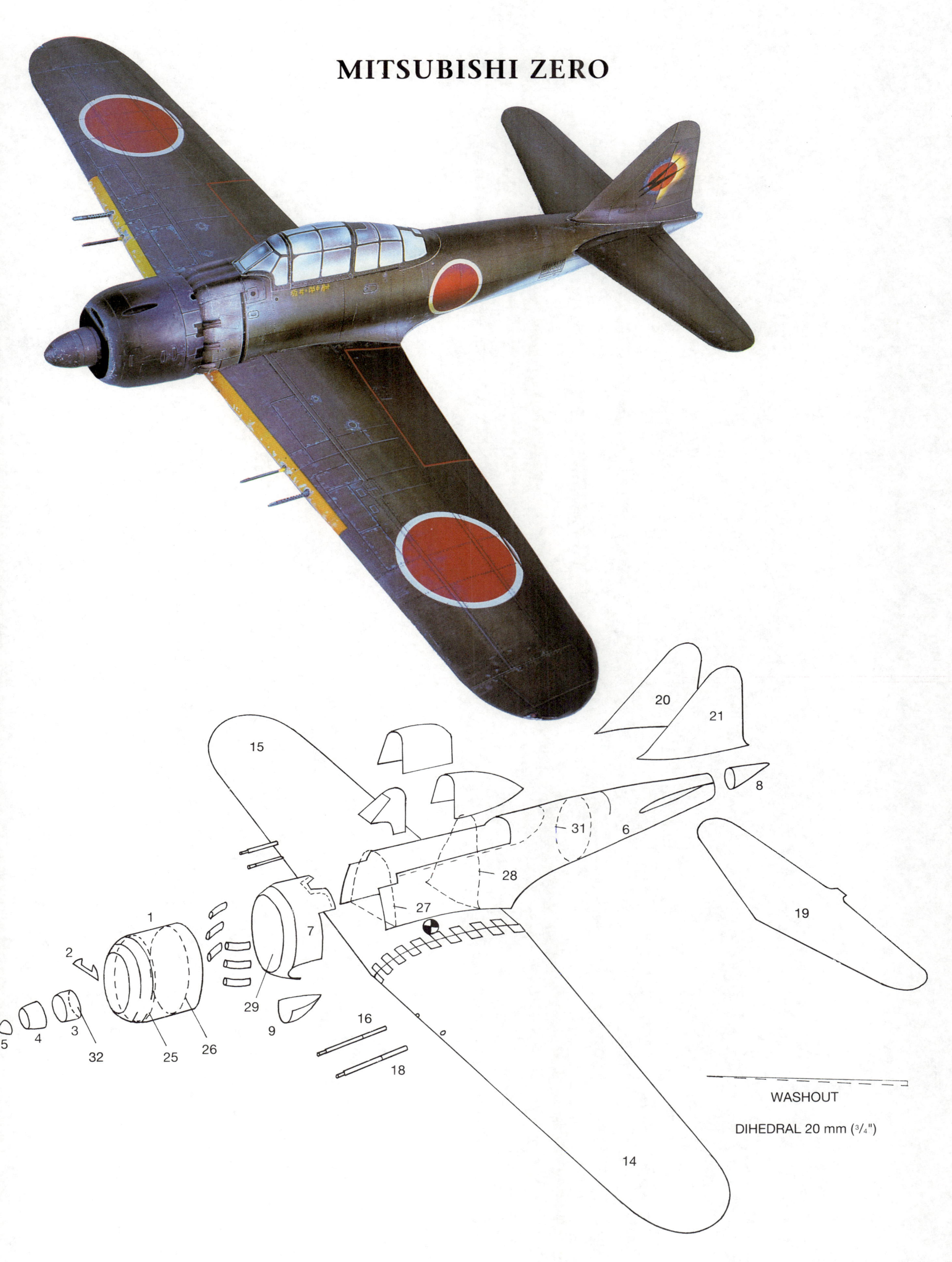

MESSERSCHMITT BF.109E

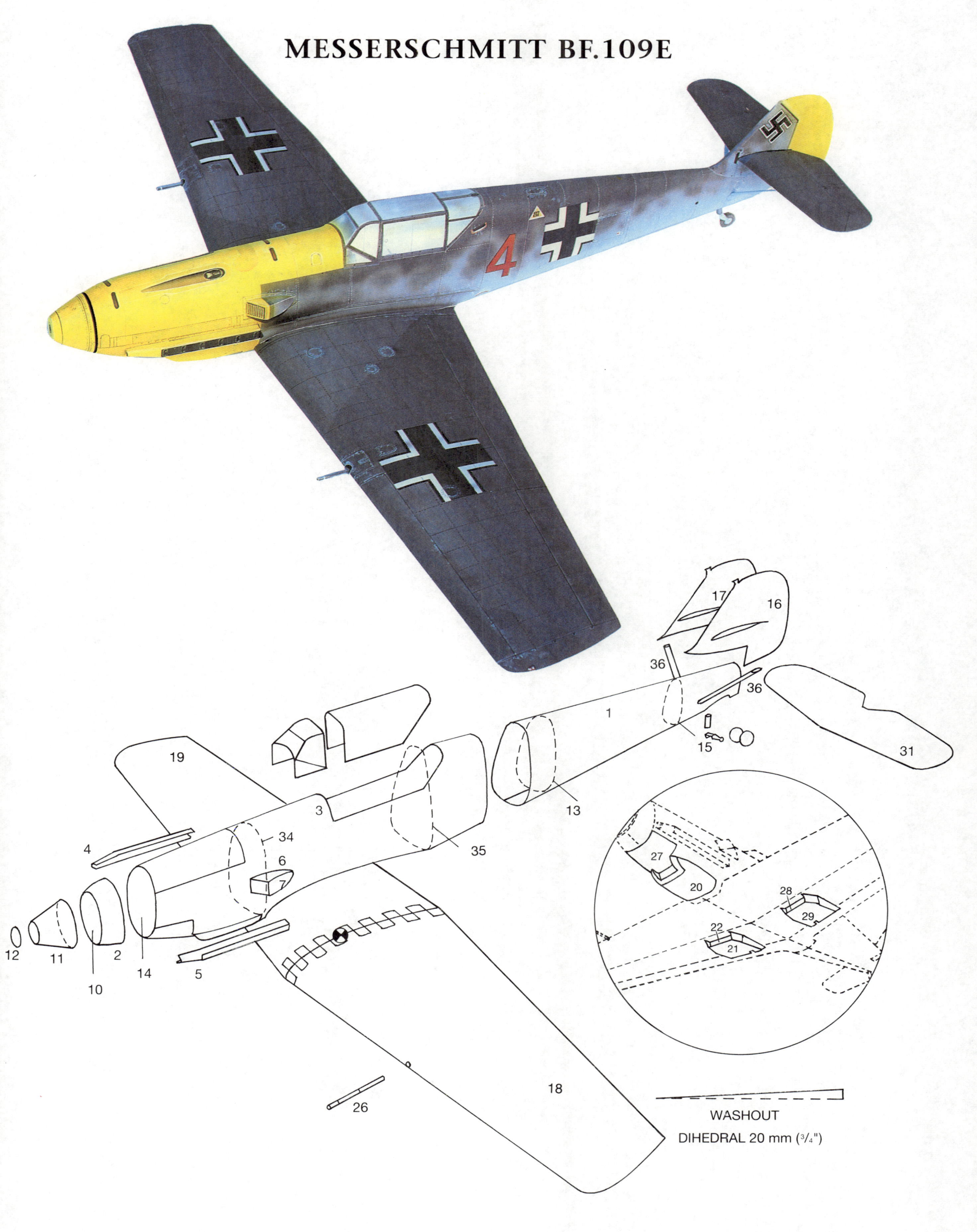

FAIREY BARRACUDA

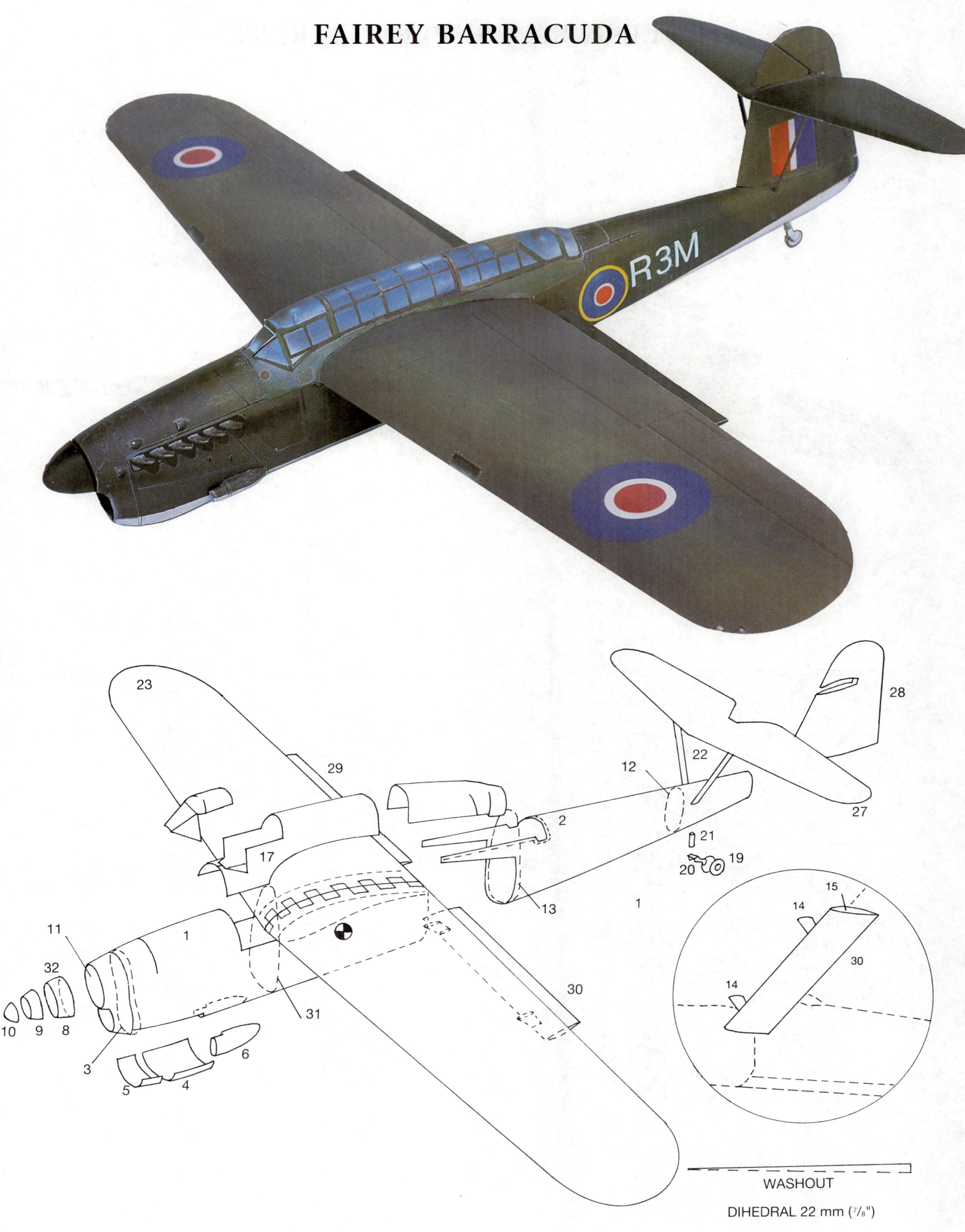

BOEING B.52 SUPERFORTRESS

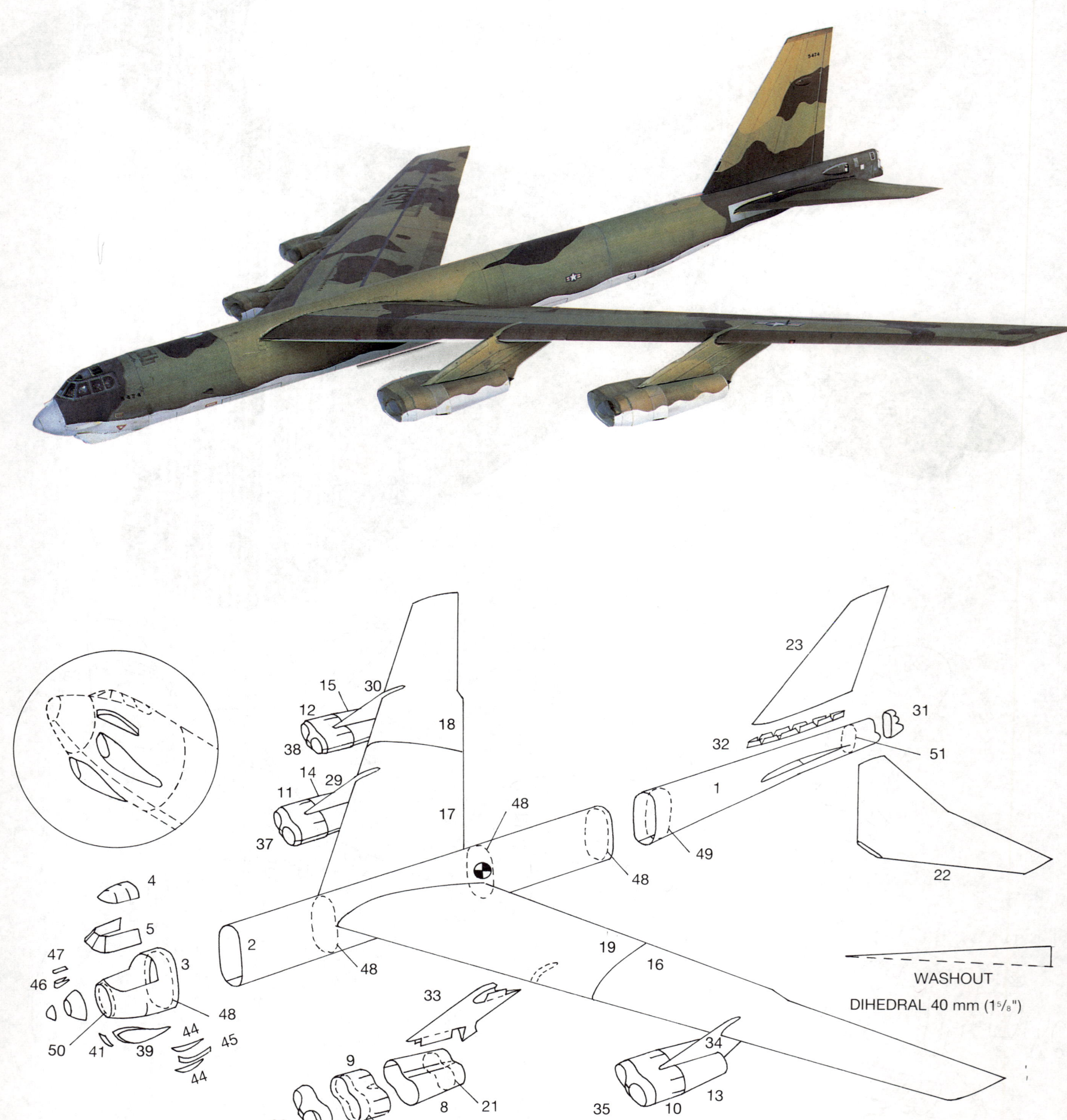

BOEING B.52 SUPERFORTRESS

LOCKHEED U.2R

LOCKHEED U.2R

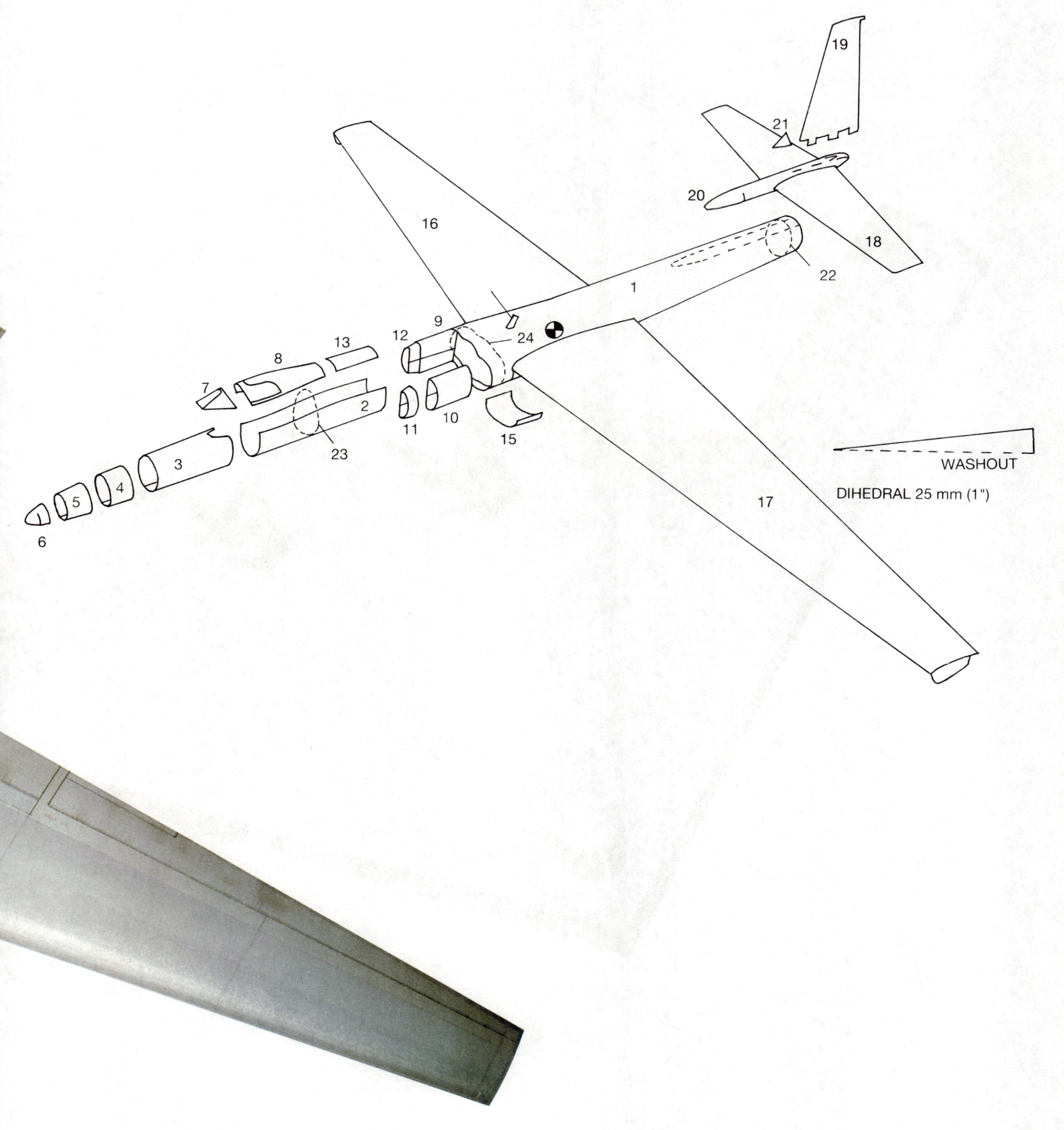

NORTHROP B.2 'STEALTH' BOMBER

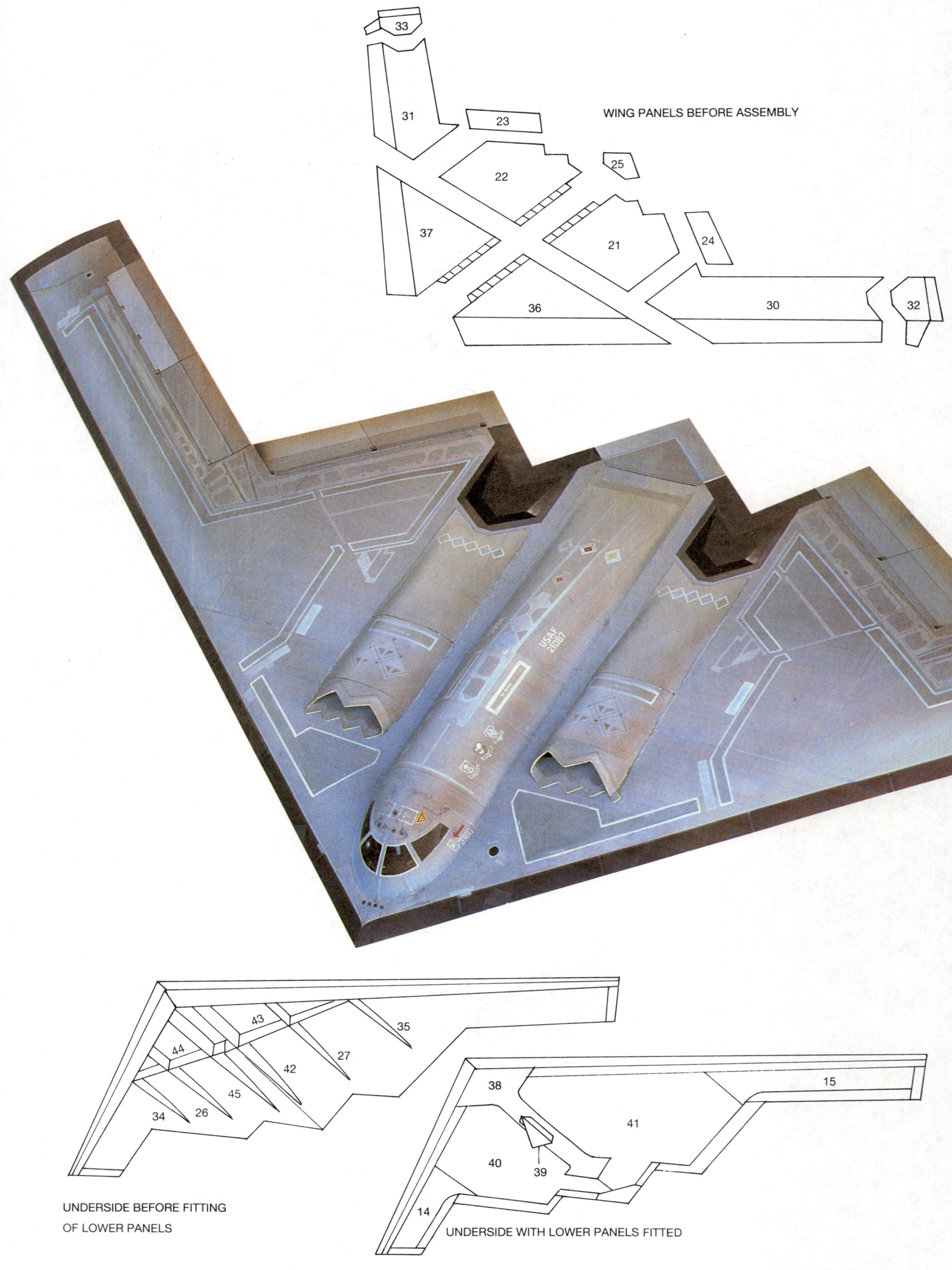

NORTHROP B.2 'STEALTH' BOMBER

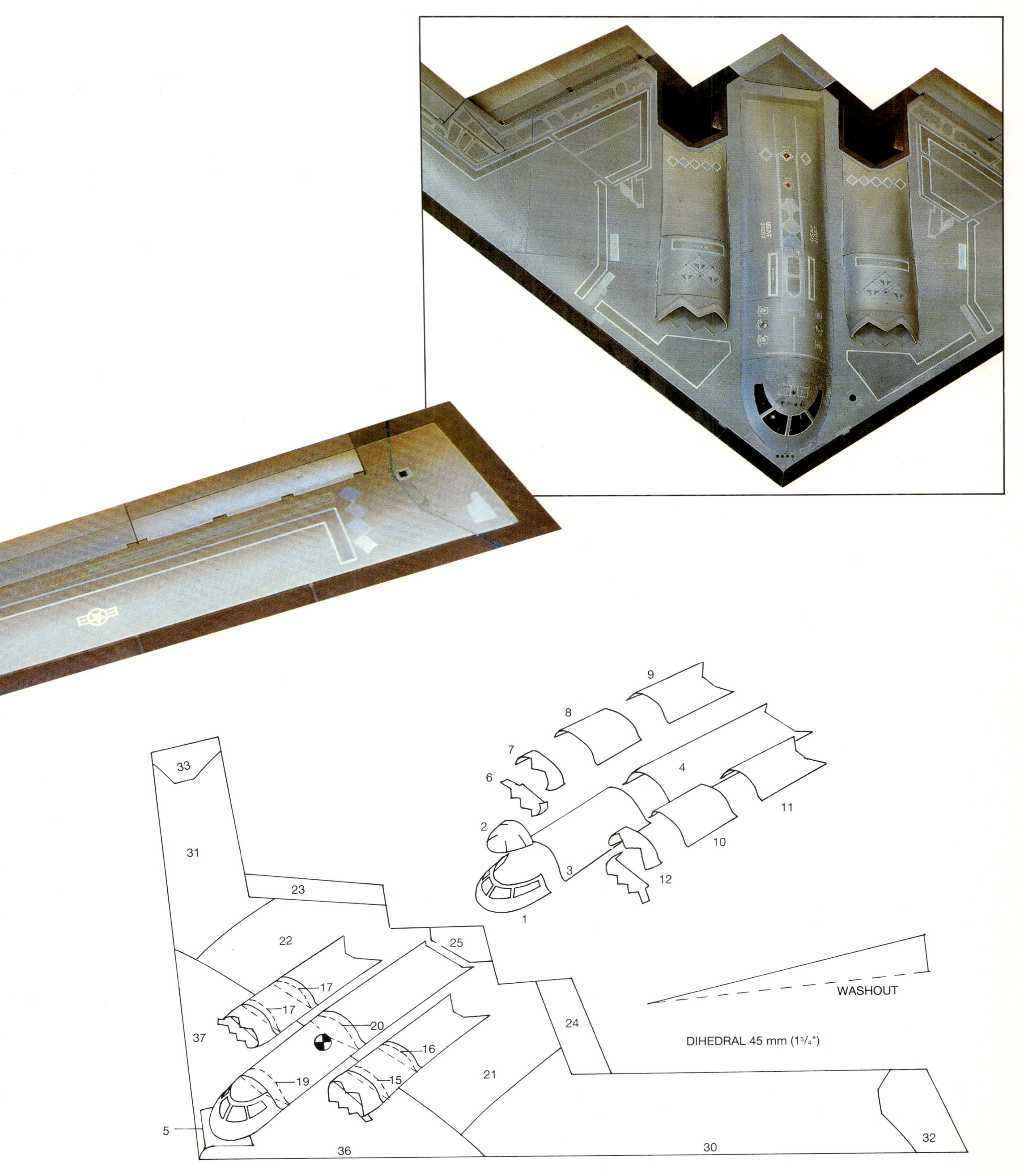

Press-out Parts

For general construction advice, please refer to the Introduction.

Approximate wing spans of planes

Gloster Gladiator 540 mm (21")
Hawker Hurricane 500 mm (20")
Mitsubishi Zero 640 mm (25")
Messerschmitt BF.109E 640 mm (25")
Fairey Barracuda 640 mm (25")
Boeing B.52 Superfortress 920 mm (36")
Lockheed U.2R 640 mm (25")
Northrop B.2 'Stealth' Bomber 1,220 mm (48")

K7967

K7967

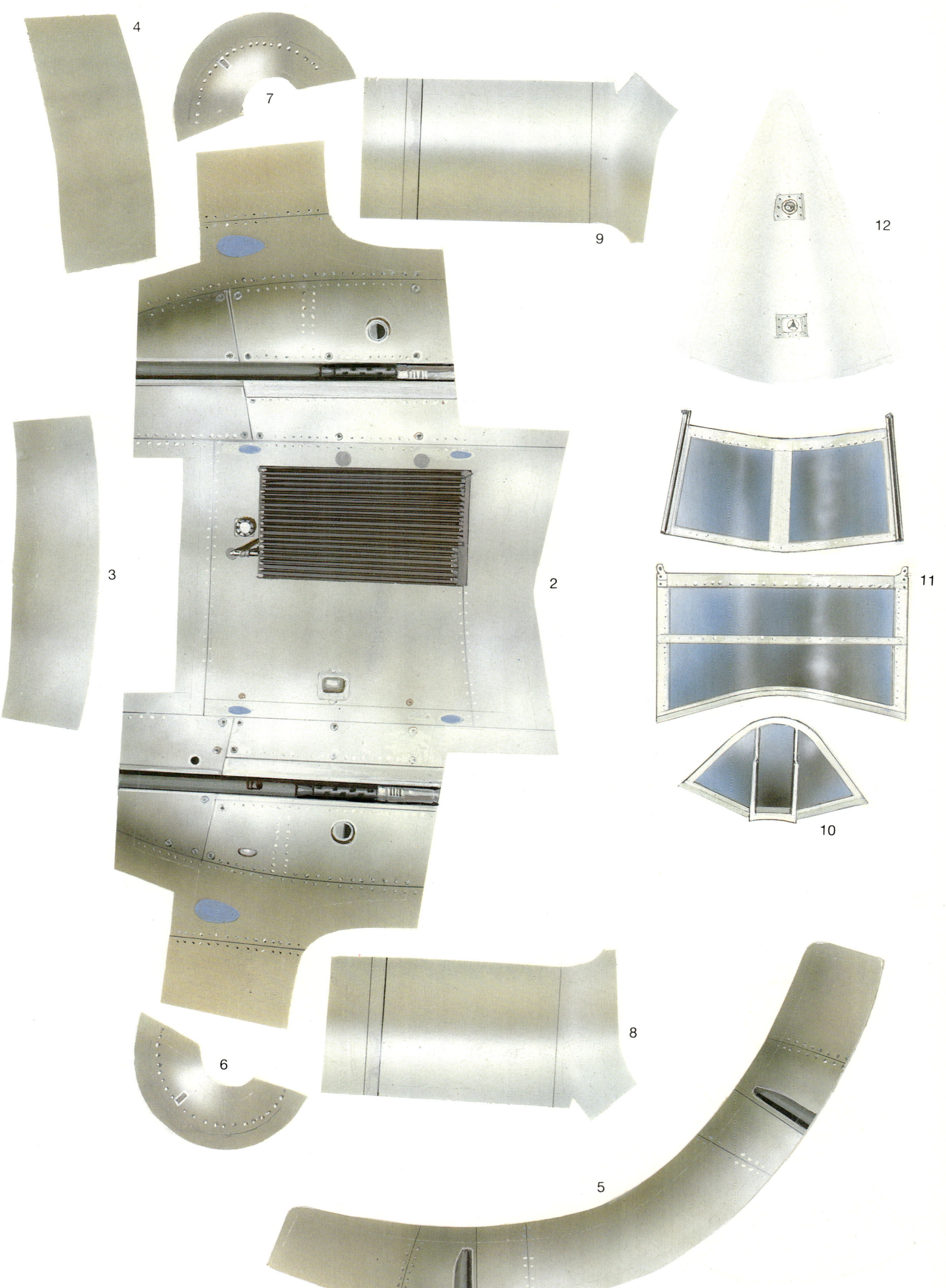

4
7
9
12
11
3
2
10
8
6
5

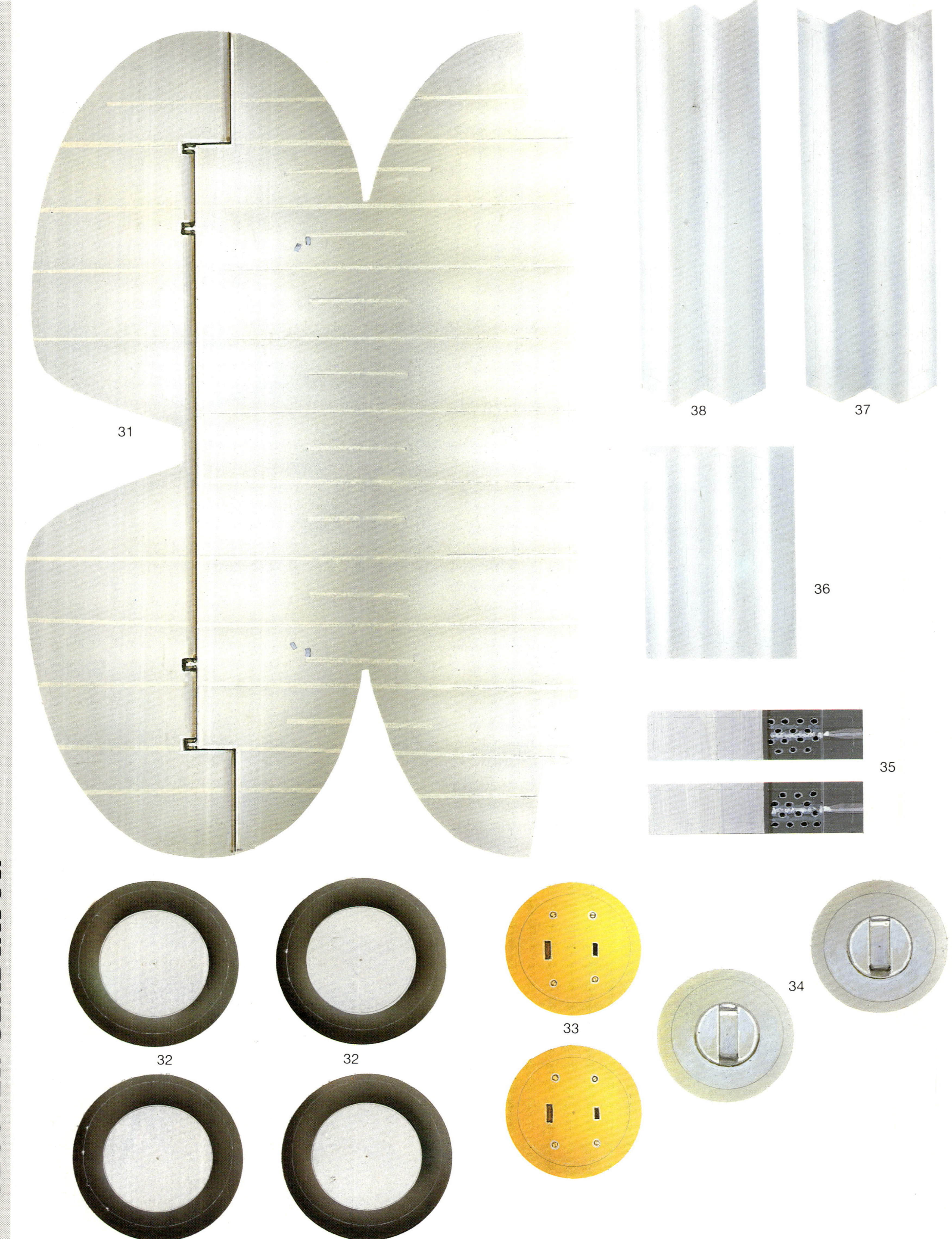
31
32
32
33
34
35
36
37
38

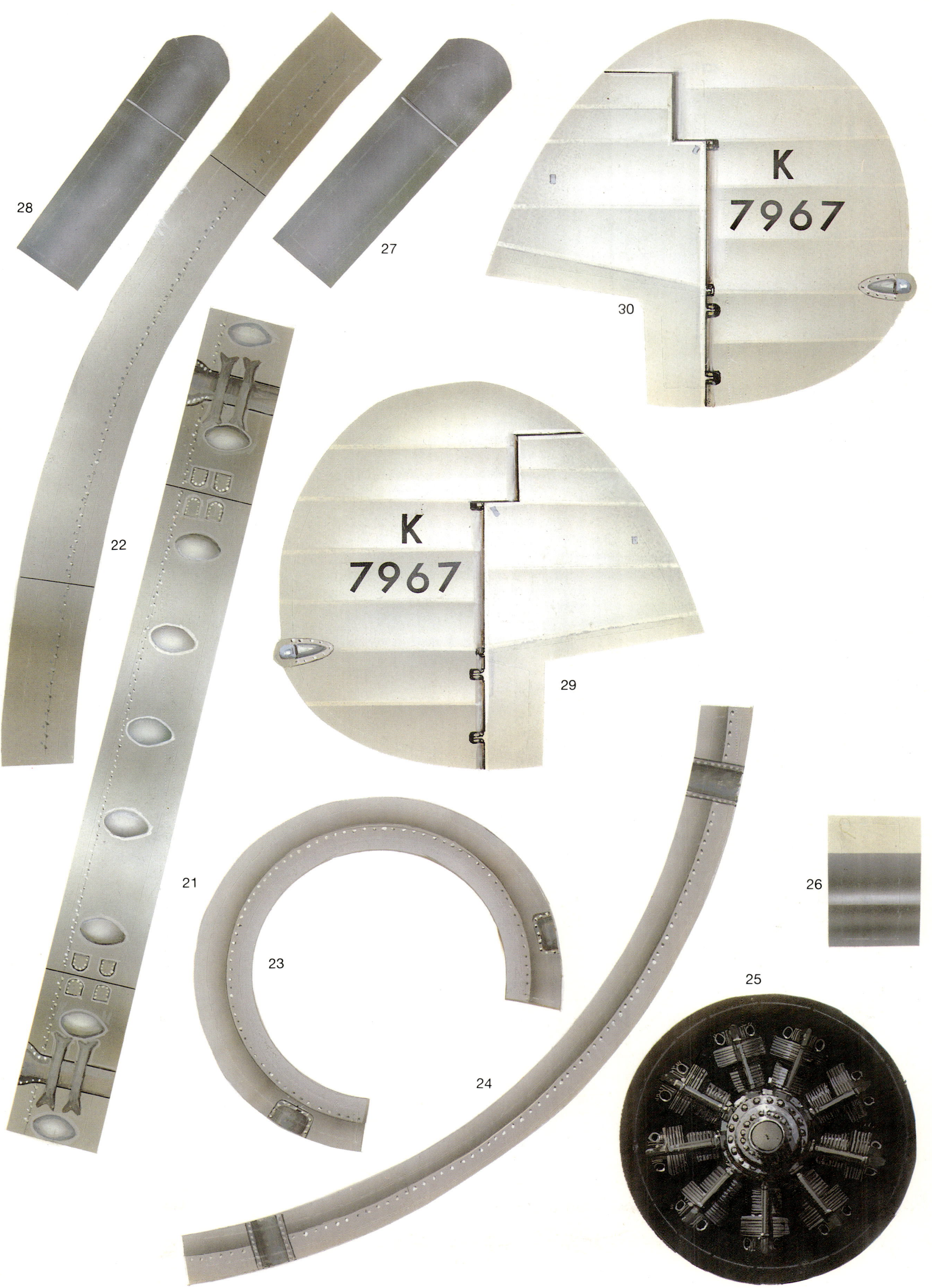
28
27
30
K 7967
K 7967
29
22
21
23
24
26
25

39

40

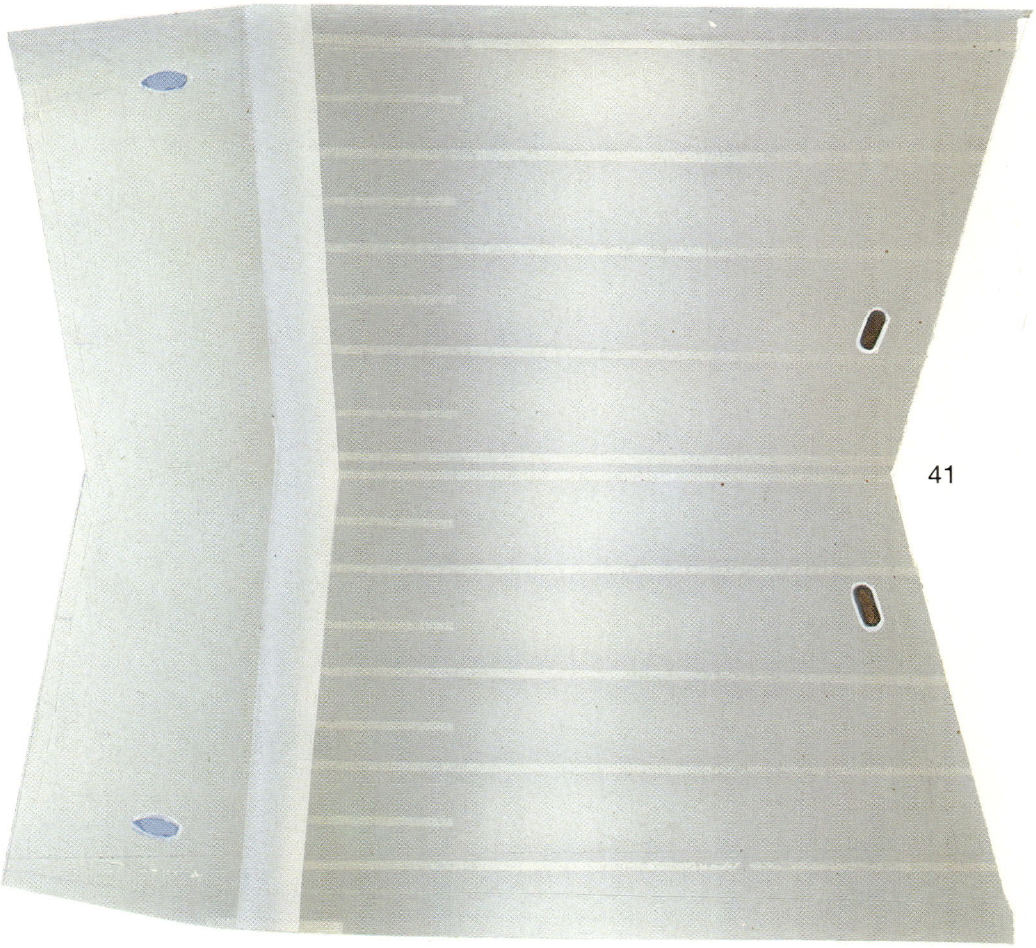

41

42

43

44

45
46

47
48

54
53
49
55
50
51
52

25

28

31

27

29

26

32

26

27

25

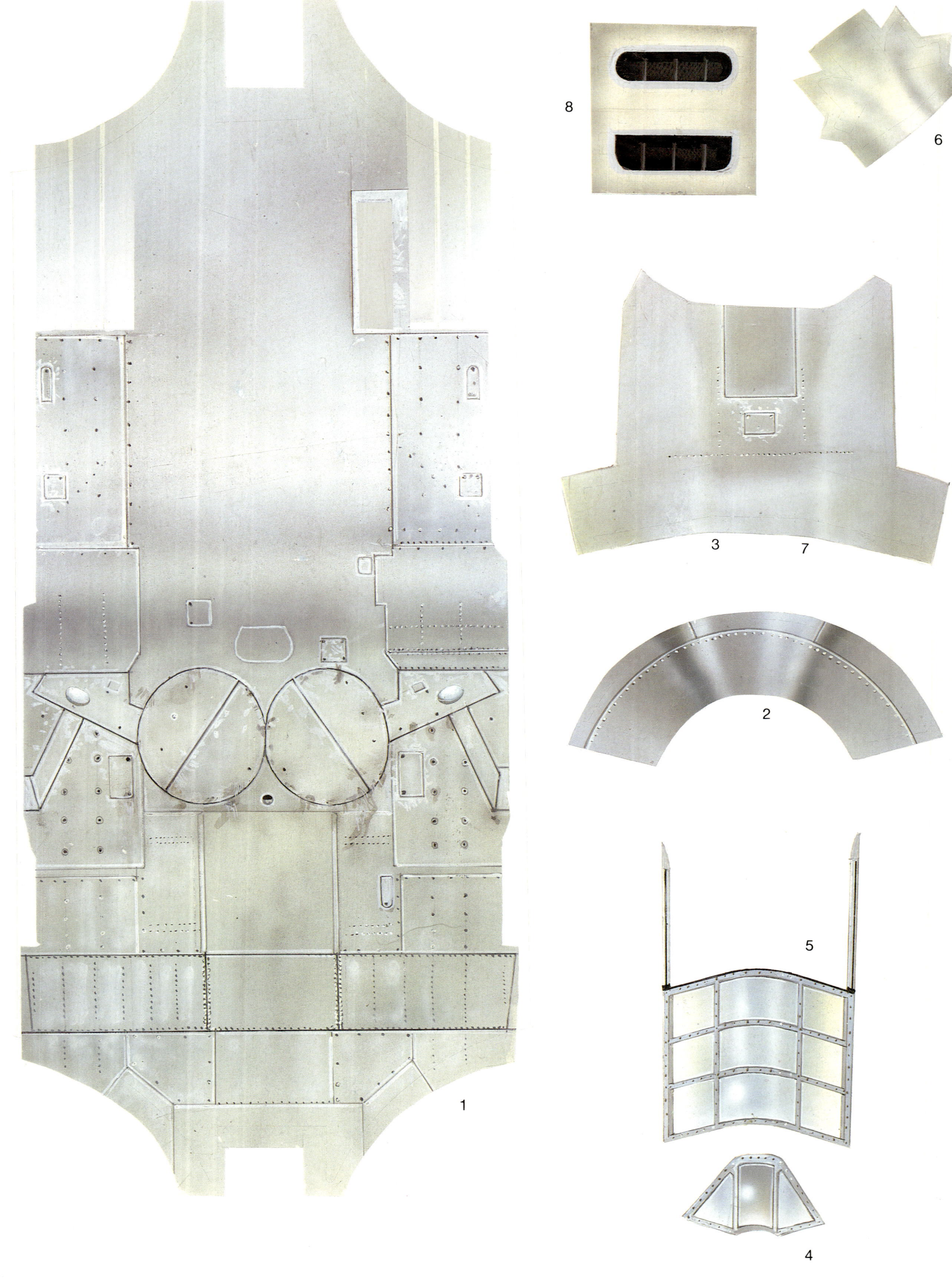

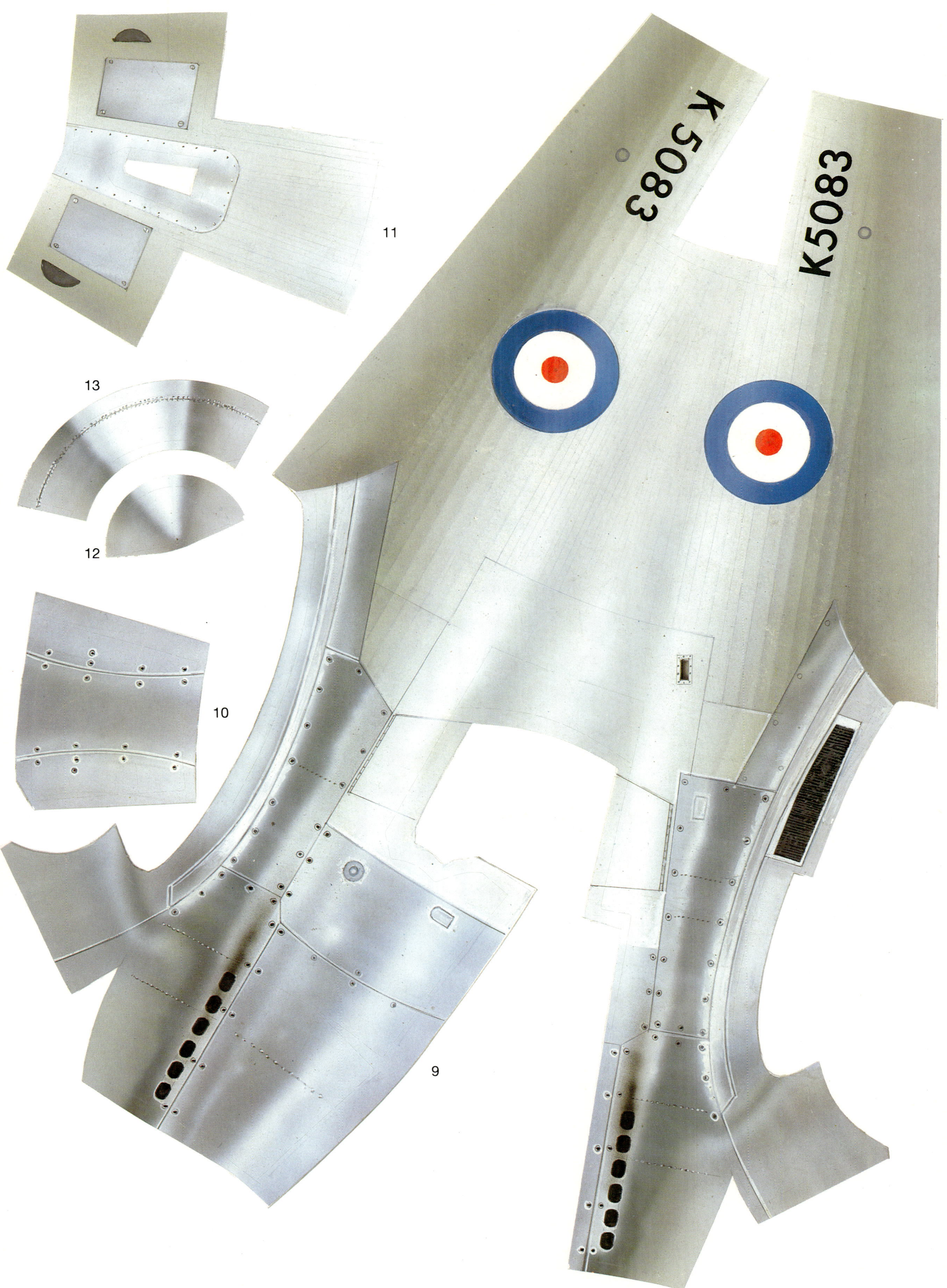

K5083
K5083
11
13
12
10
9

19

20

14

16

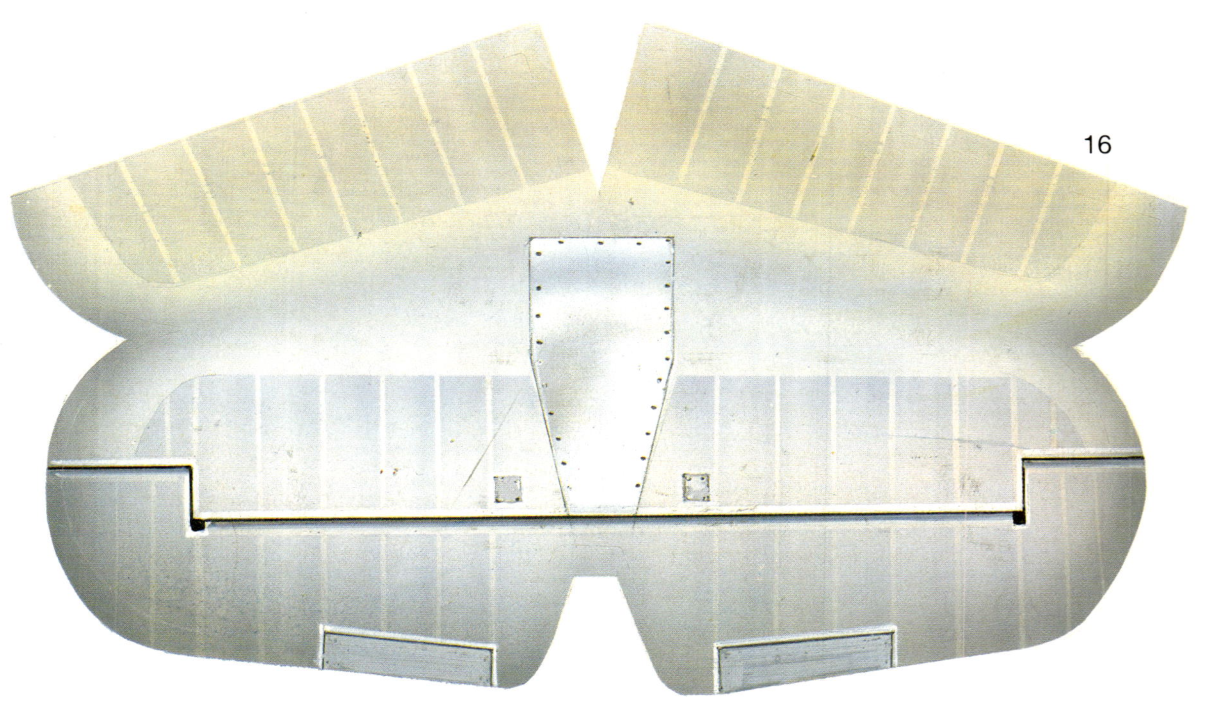

23
22
21
24
15
17
18

12
11
10
1
2
3
4
5
7
13
13

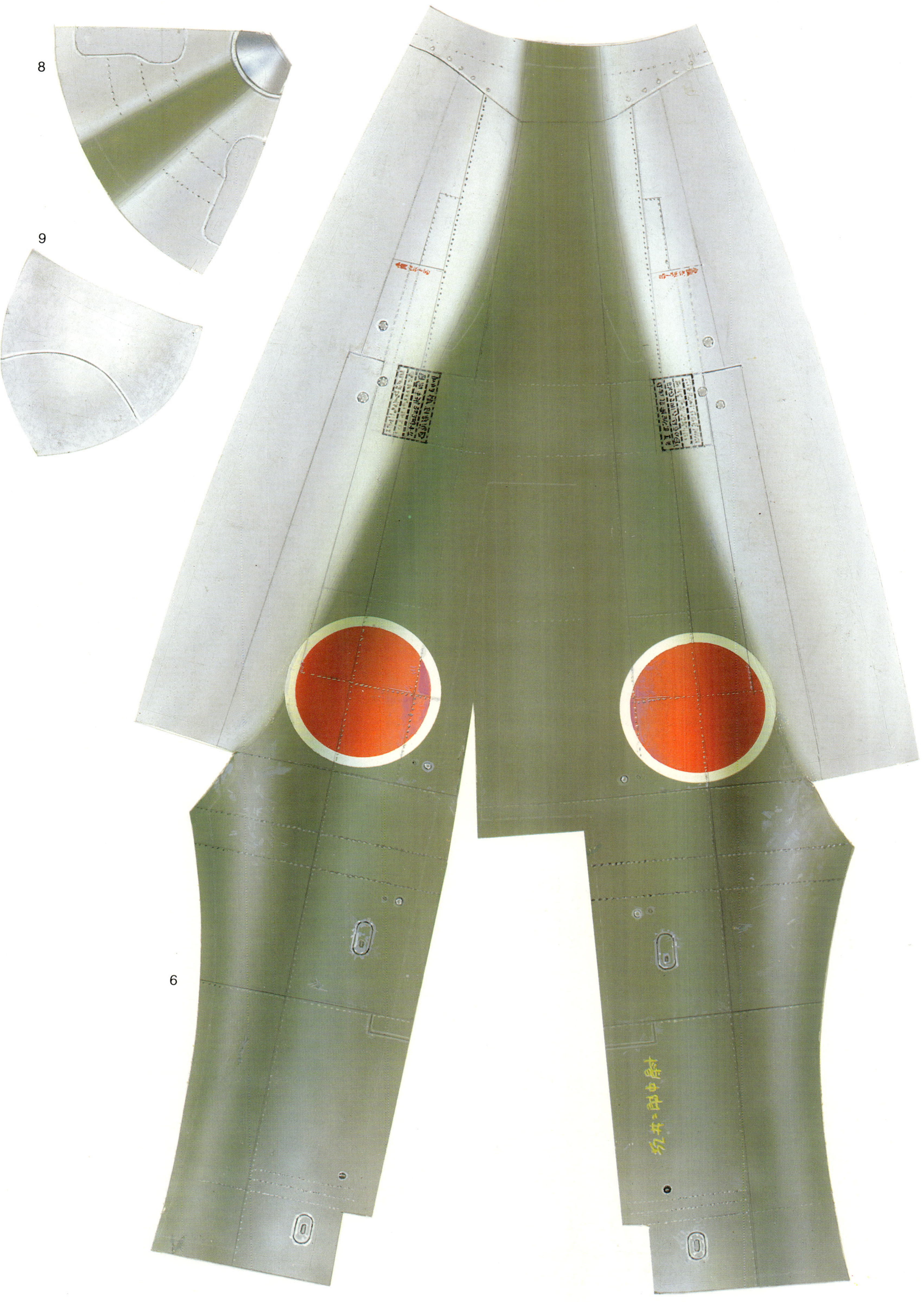

8
9
6

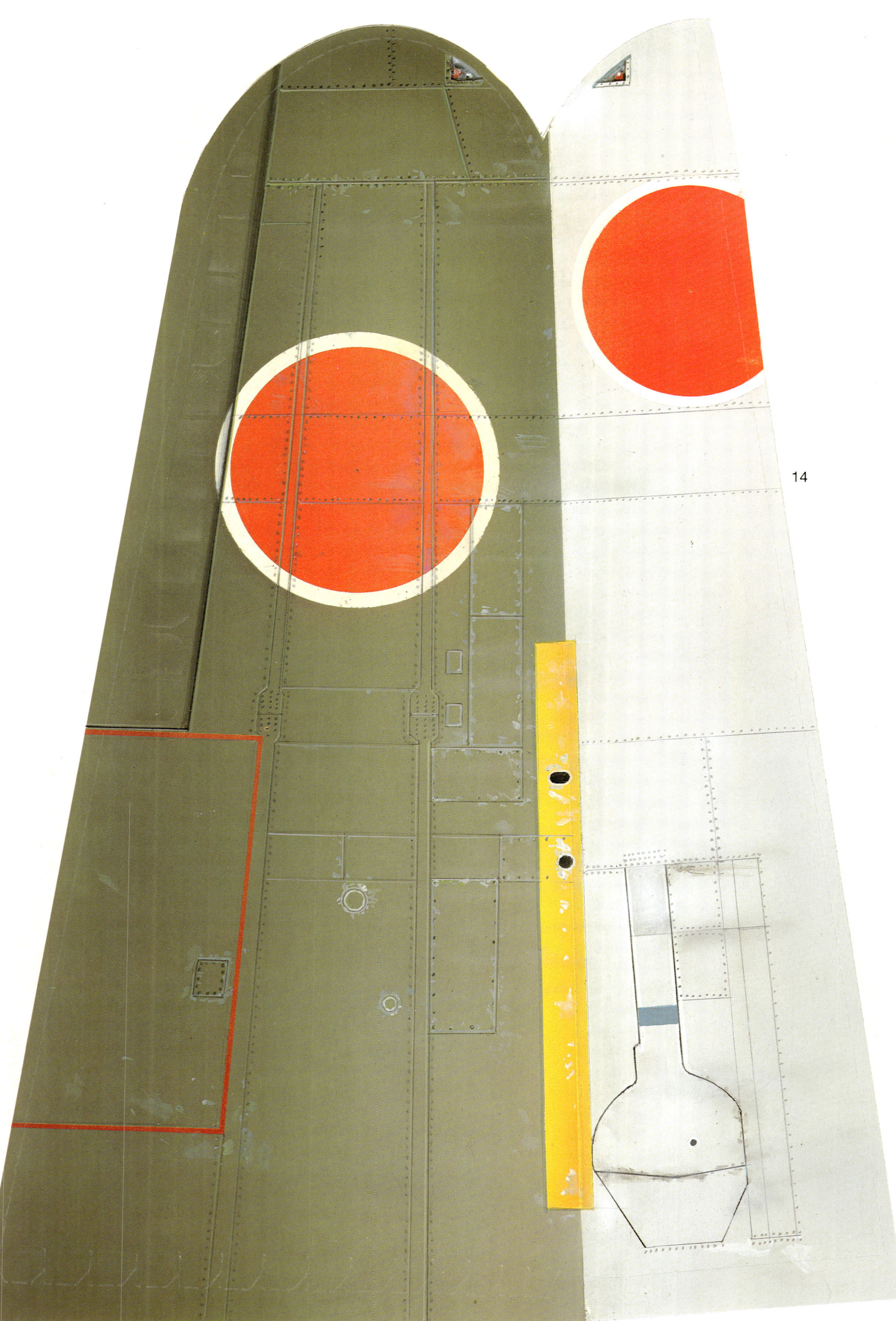
14

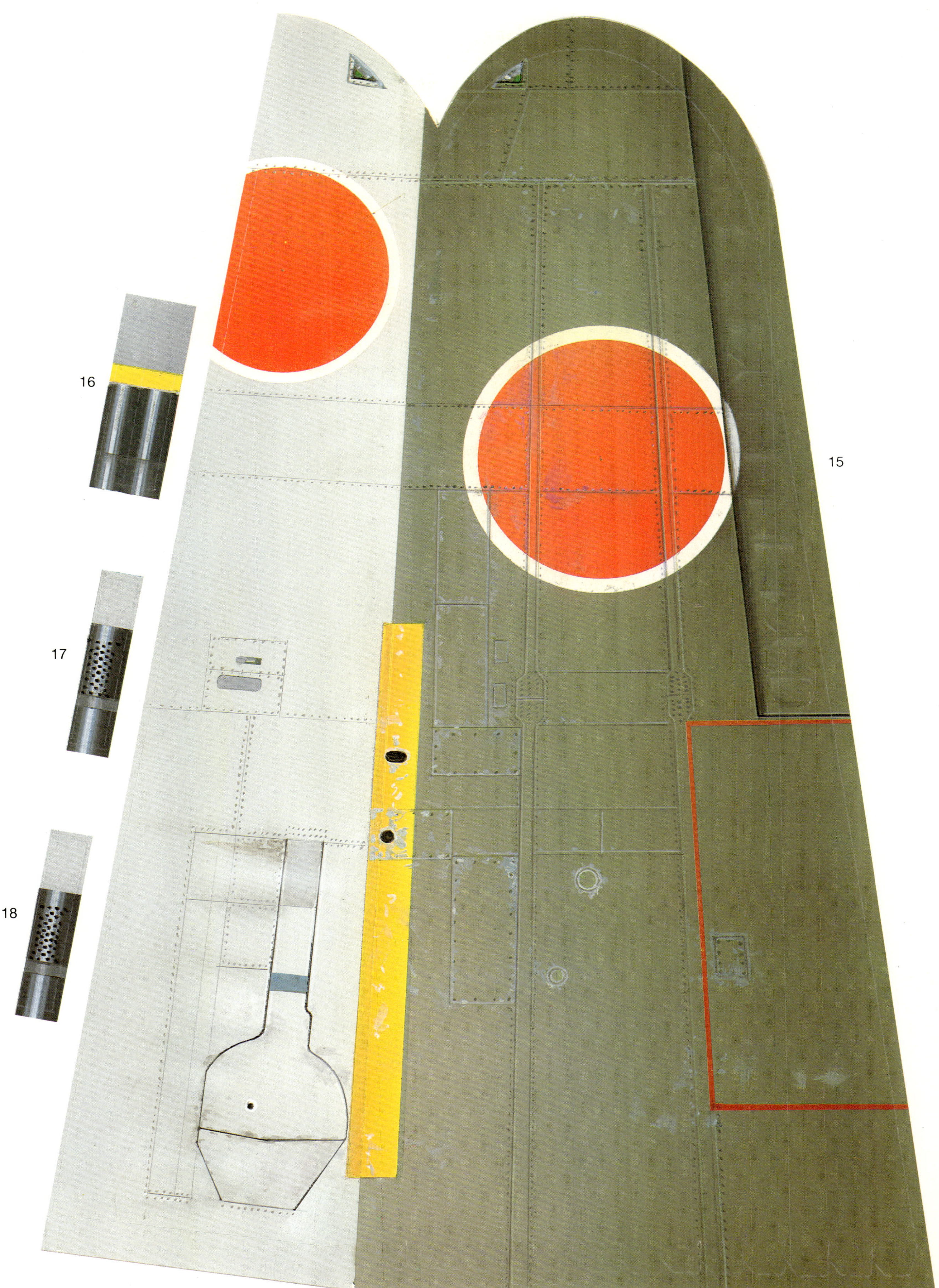

16
17
18
15

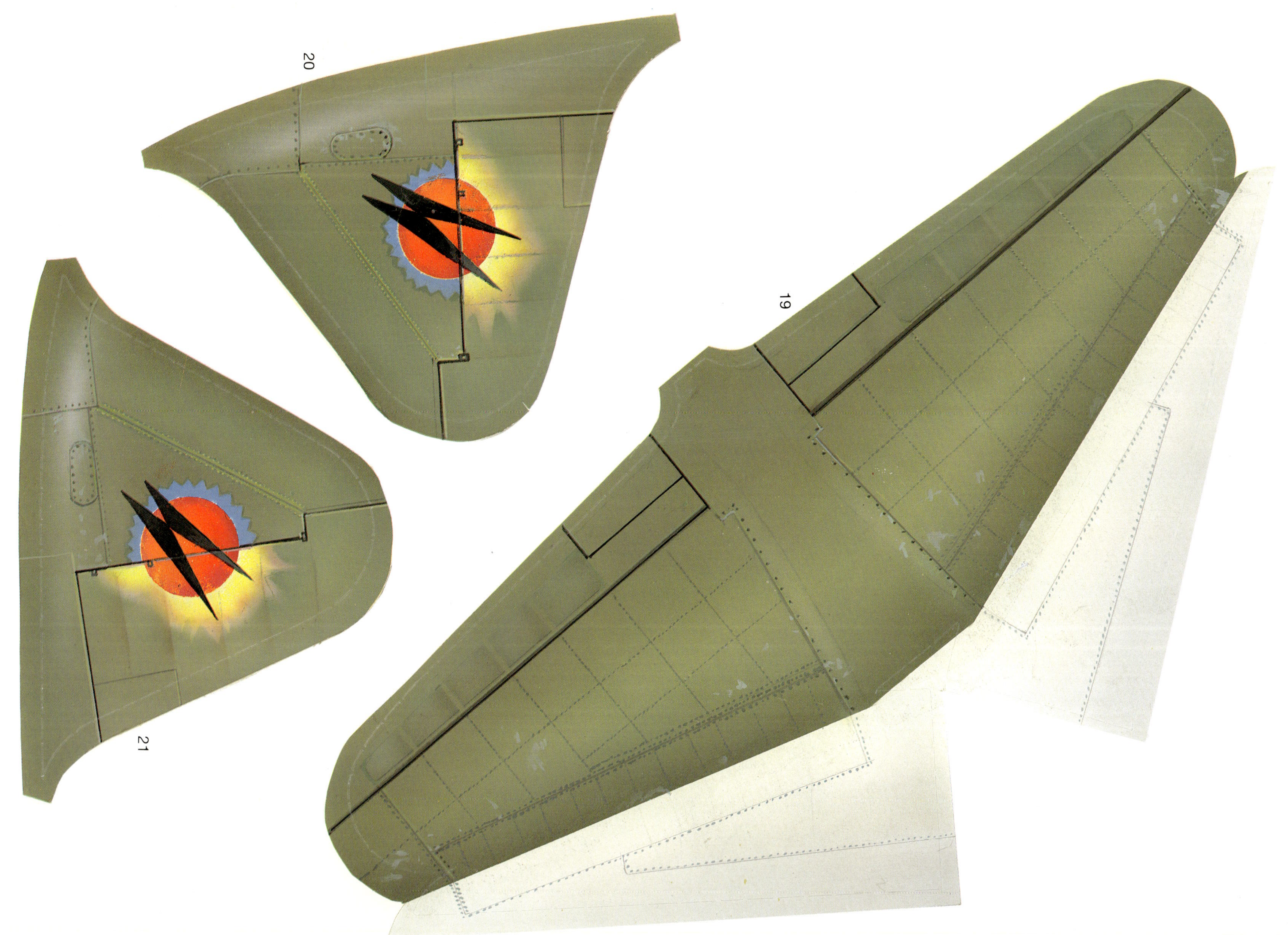

19
20
21

22

23

24

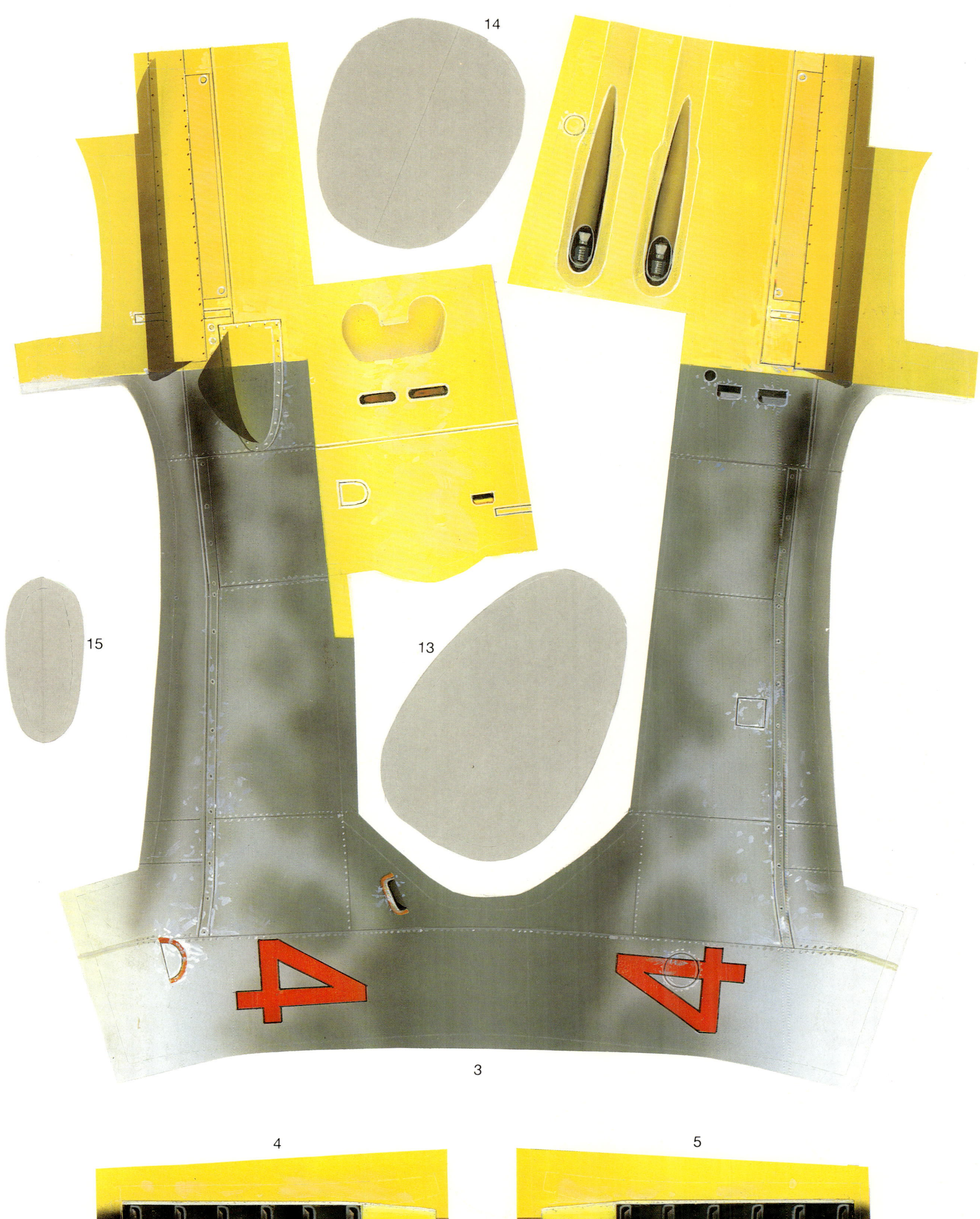

14
15
13
3
4
5

18
26
30
27
28
29

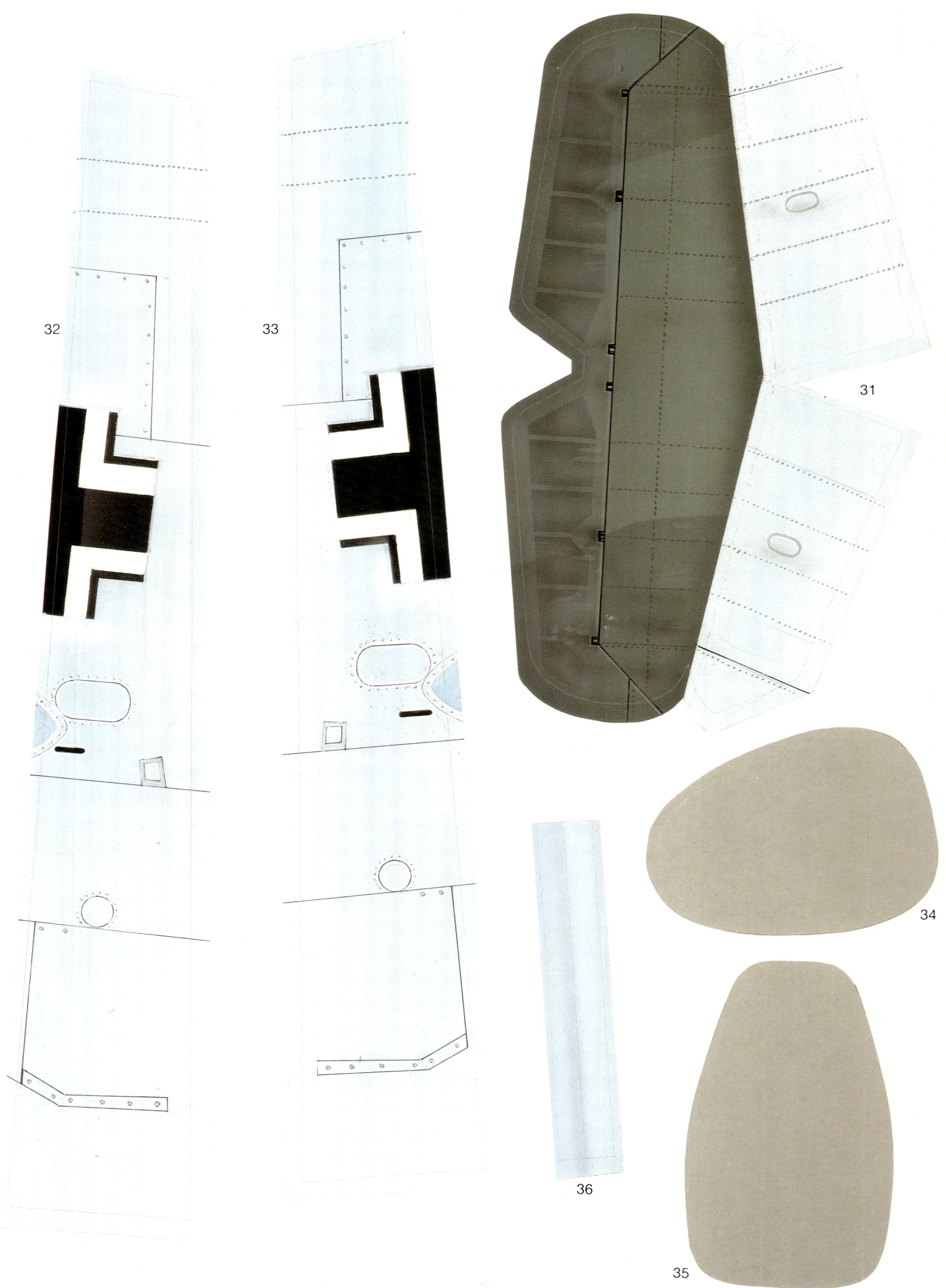
32
33
31
34
36
35

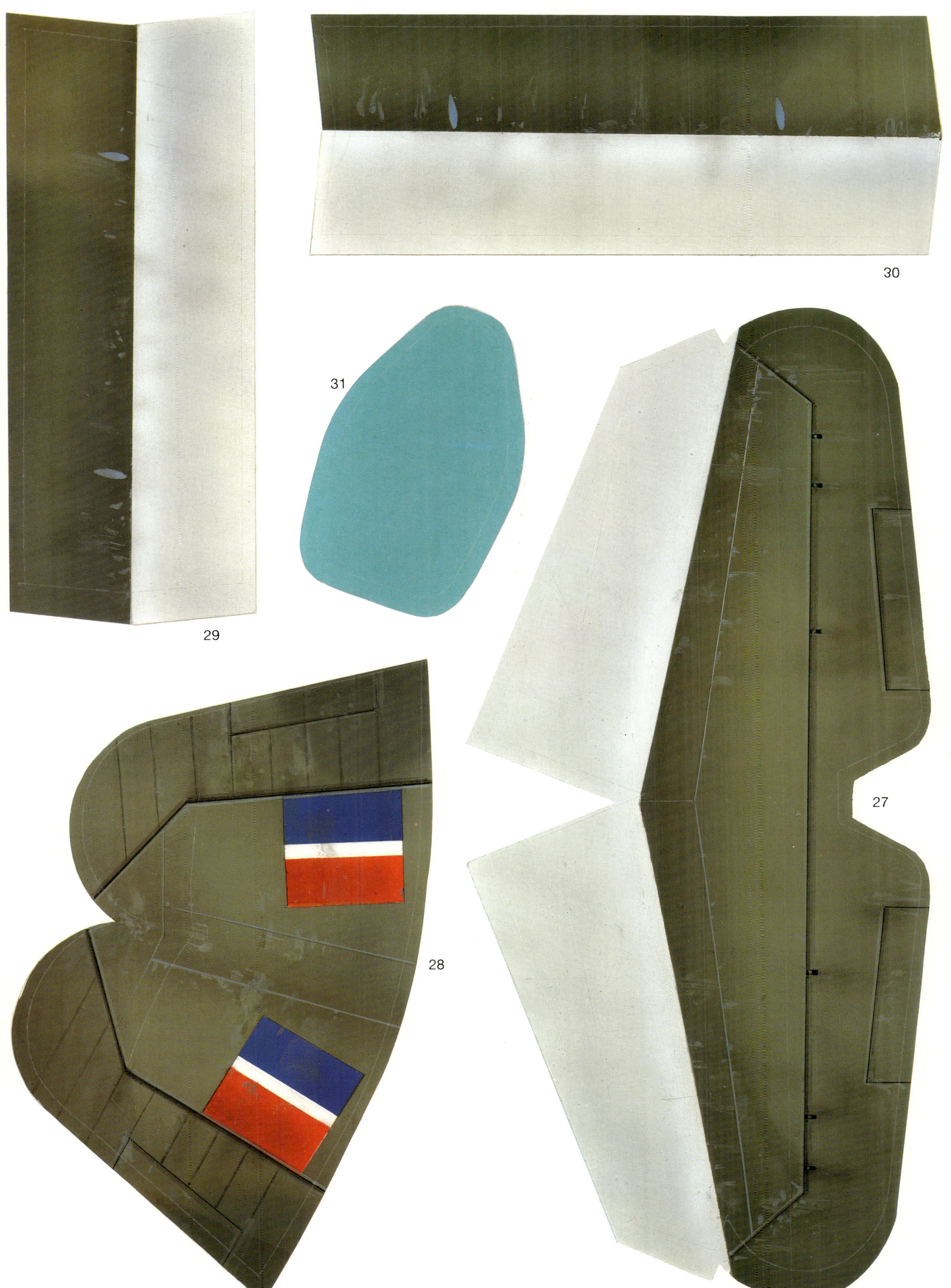

30
31
29
27
28

26
24

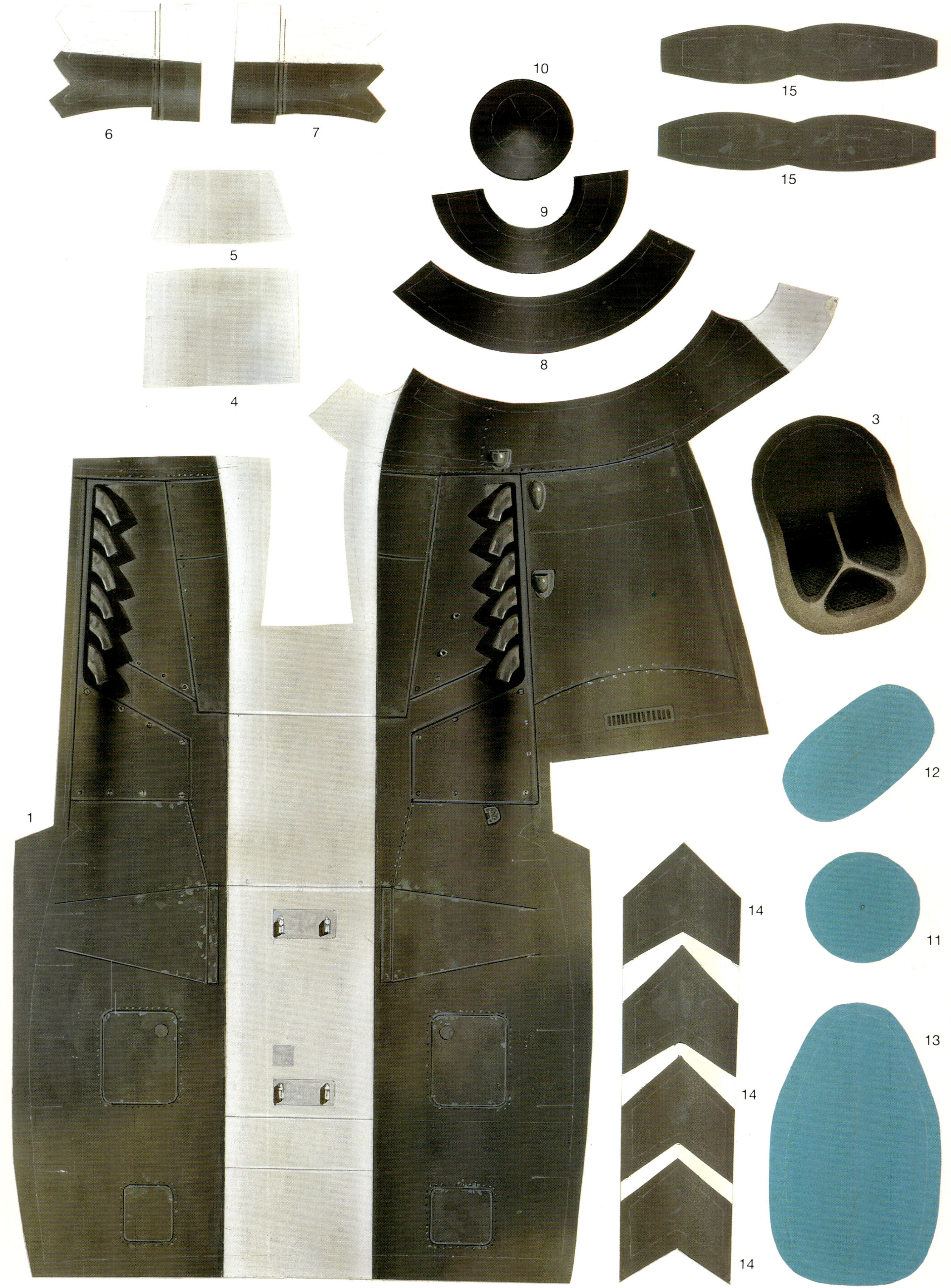

6
7
10
15
15
5
9
4
8
3
1
12
14
11
14
13
14

21
20
19
18
32
2
R3M
R3M
17
16
22

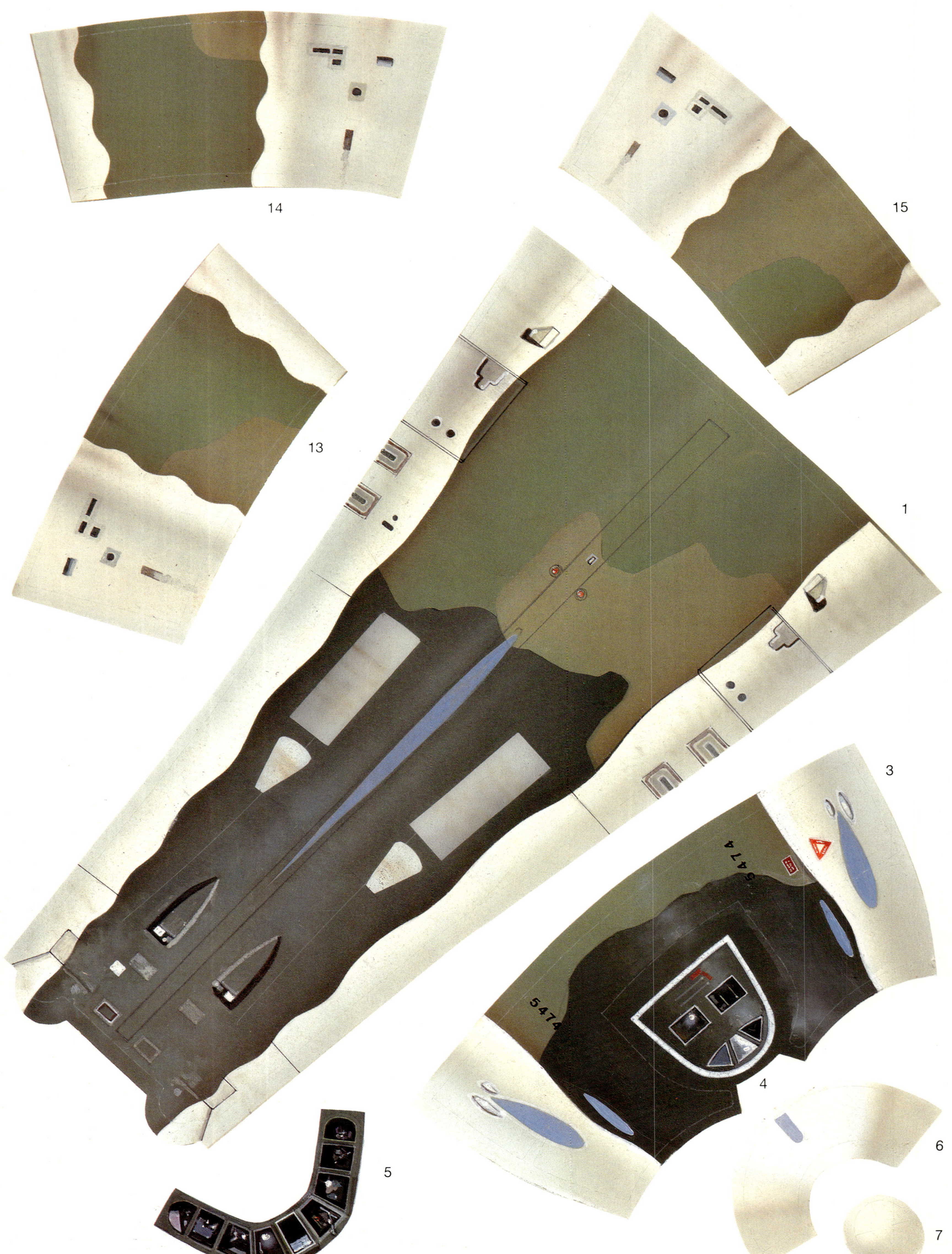

11
12
9
10
8
2

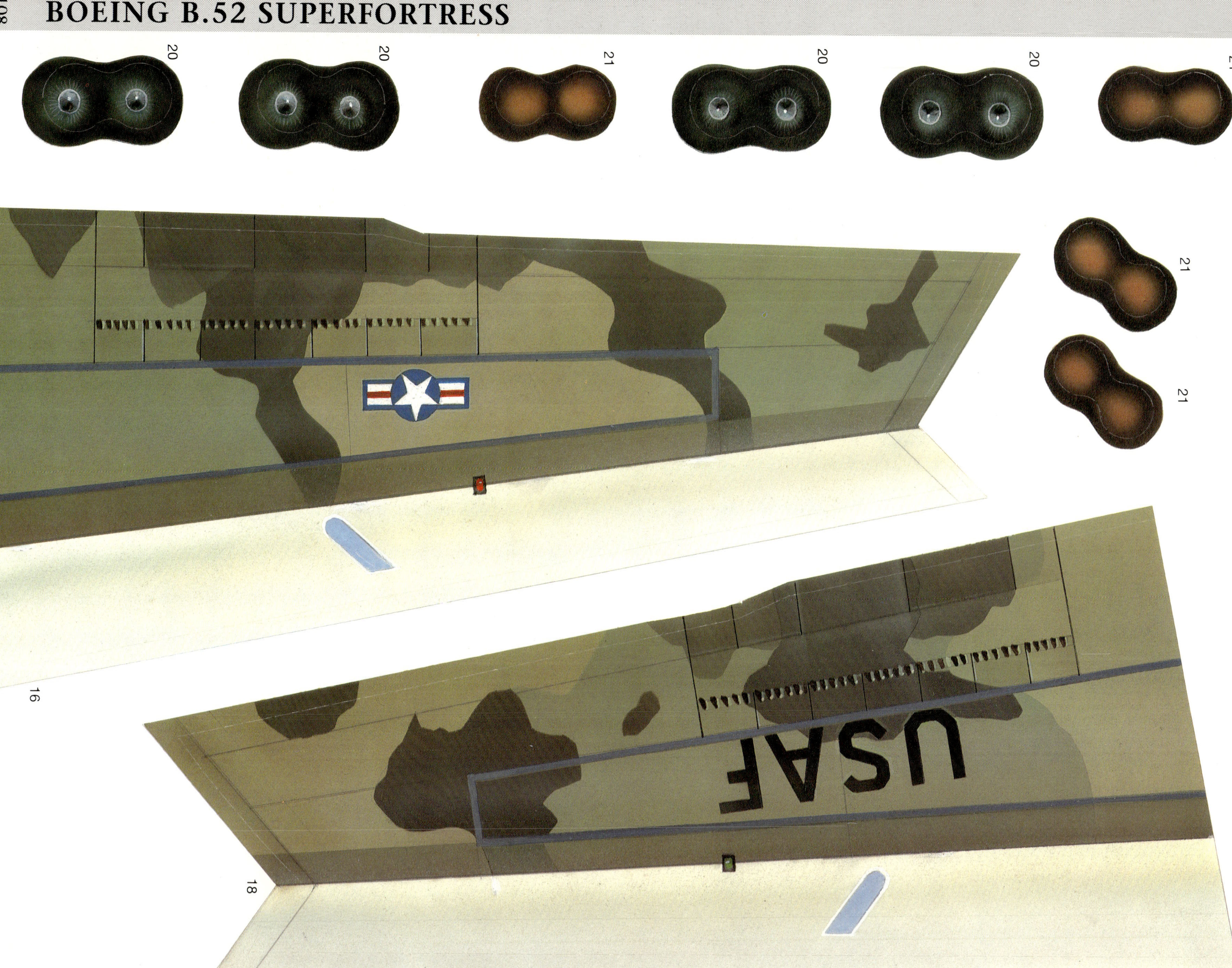
USAF

19
17

28

27

32

24

31

26

25

30
29
23
5474
5474
22

37 L
34
33
36 L
35 R
38 R
50
48
45
39 40
41 42
43
44
47
46
48
48
48
49
51

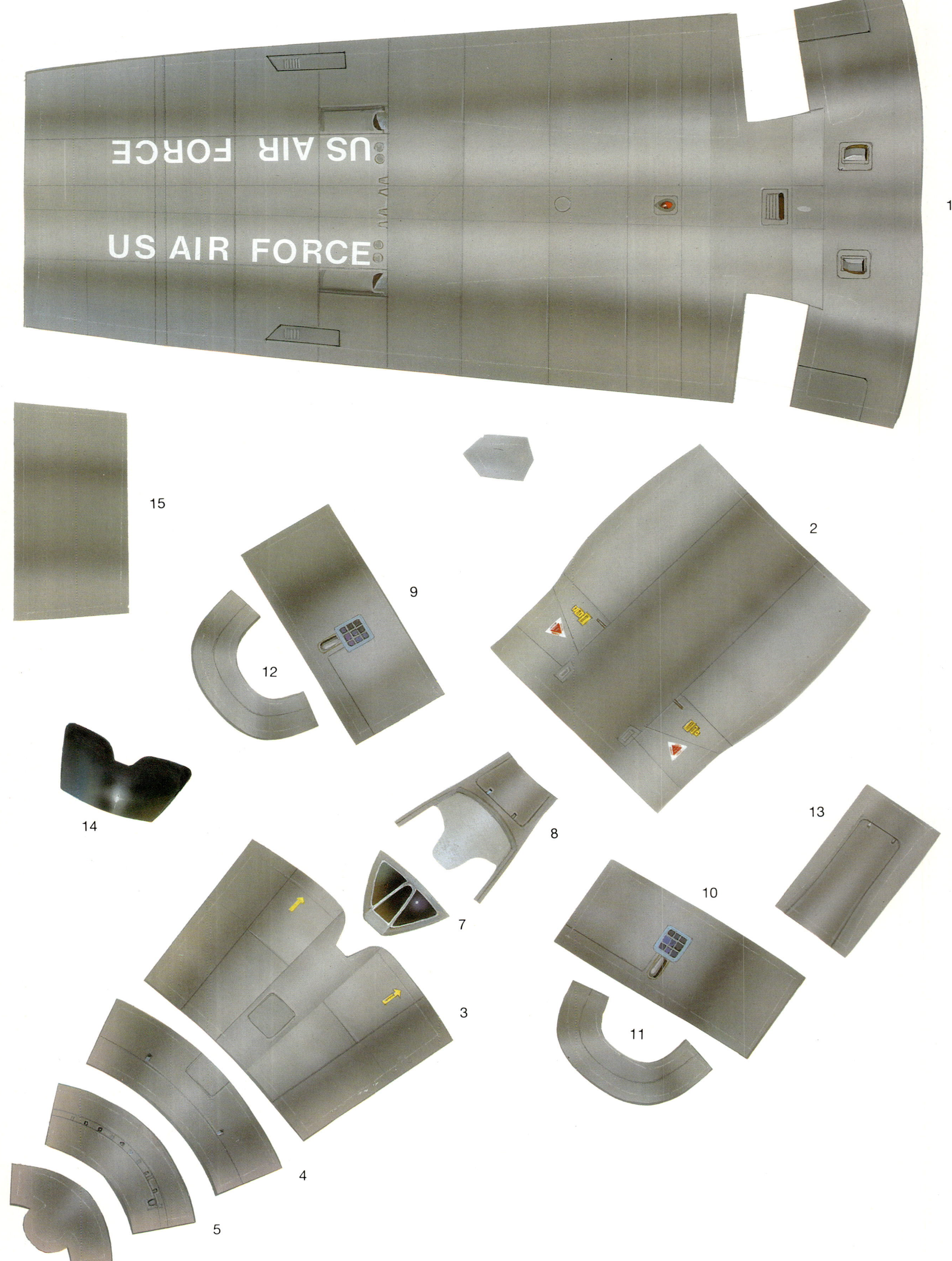

16
17
NO STEP
NO STEP
NO STEP
NO STEP
NO STEP

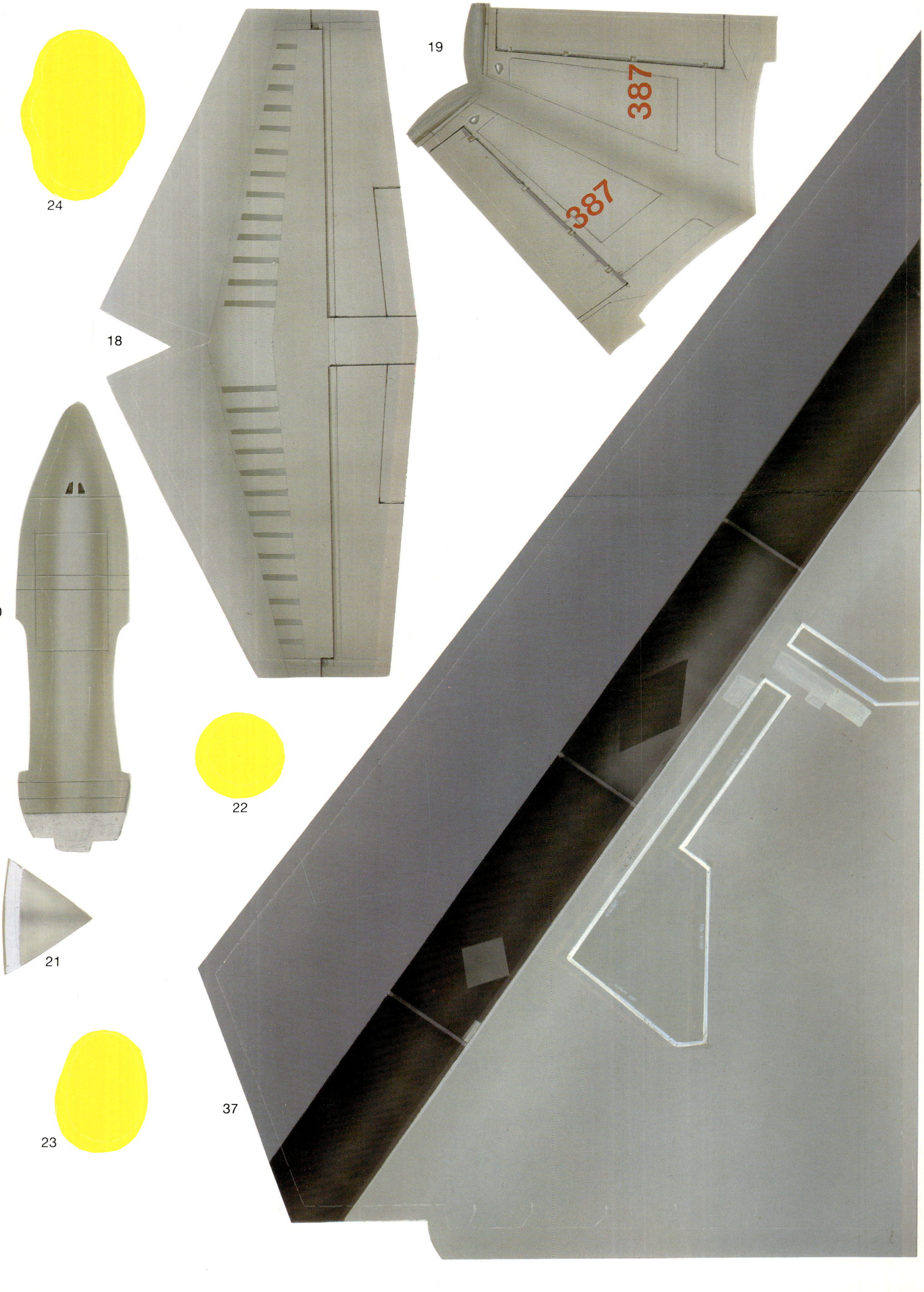

387

387

18

19

20

21

22

23

24

37

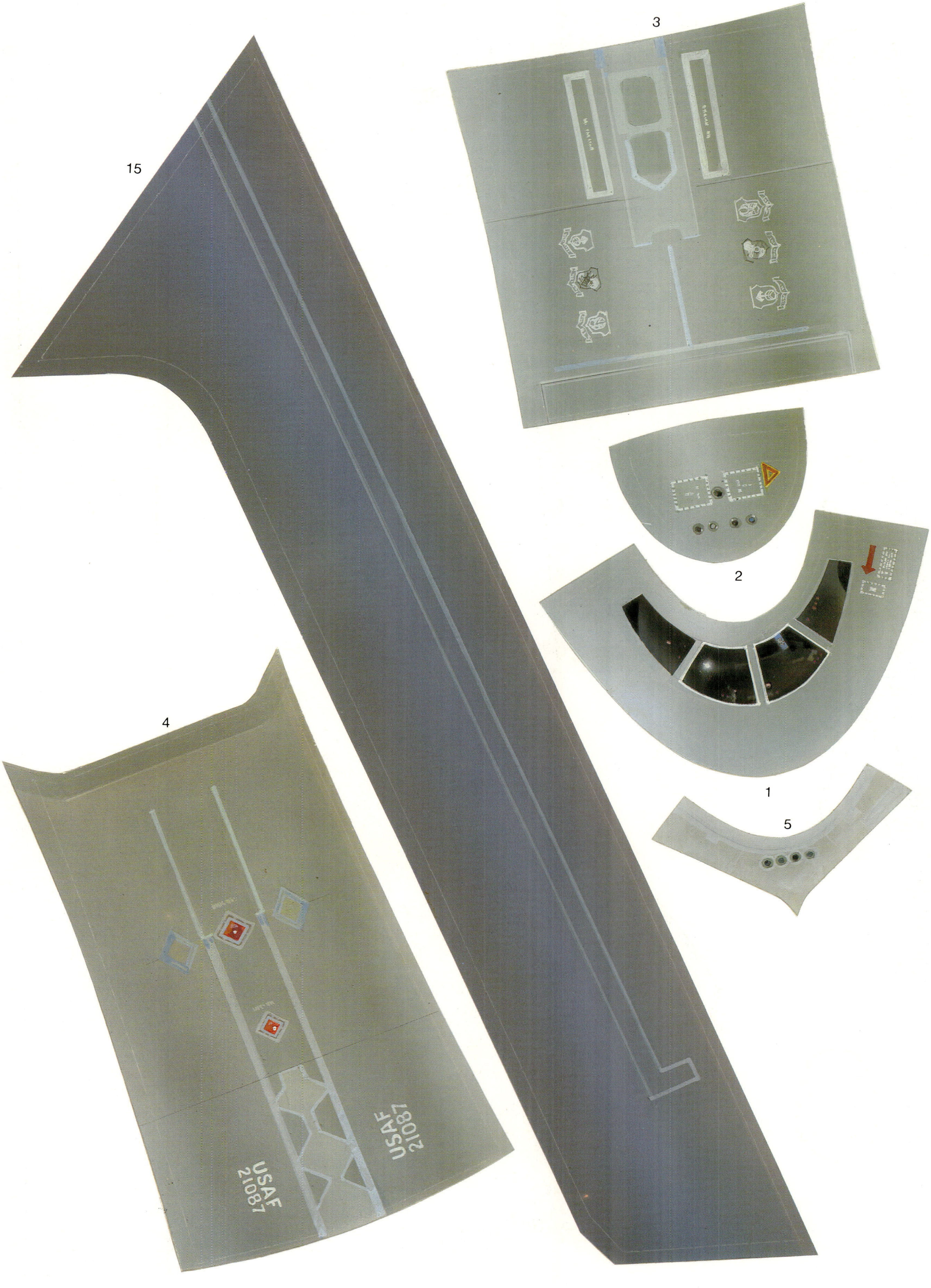

USAF
21012
USAF
21087

29
28
25
23
21

27
26
24 
22

14

13 L

11 R

10 R

12 L

20

9 L

18

19

8 L

17

7 L

16

6 R

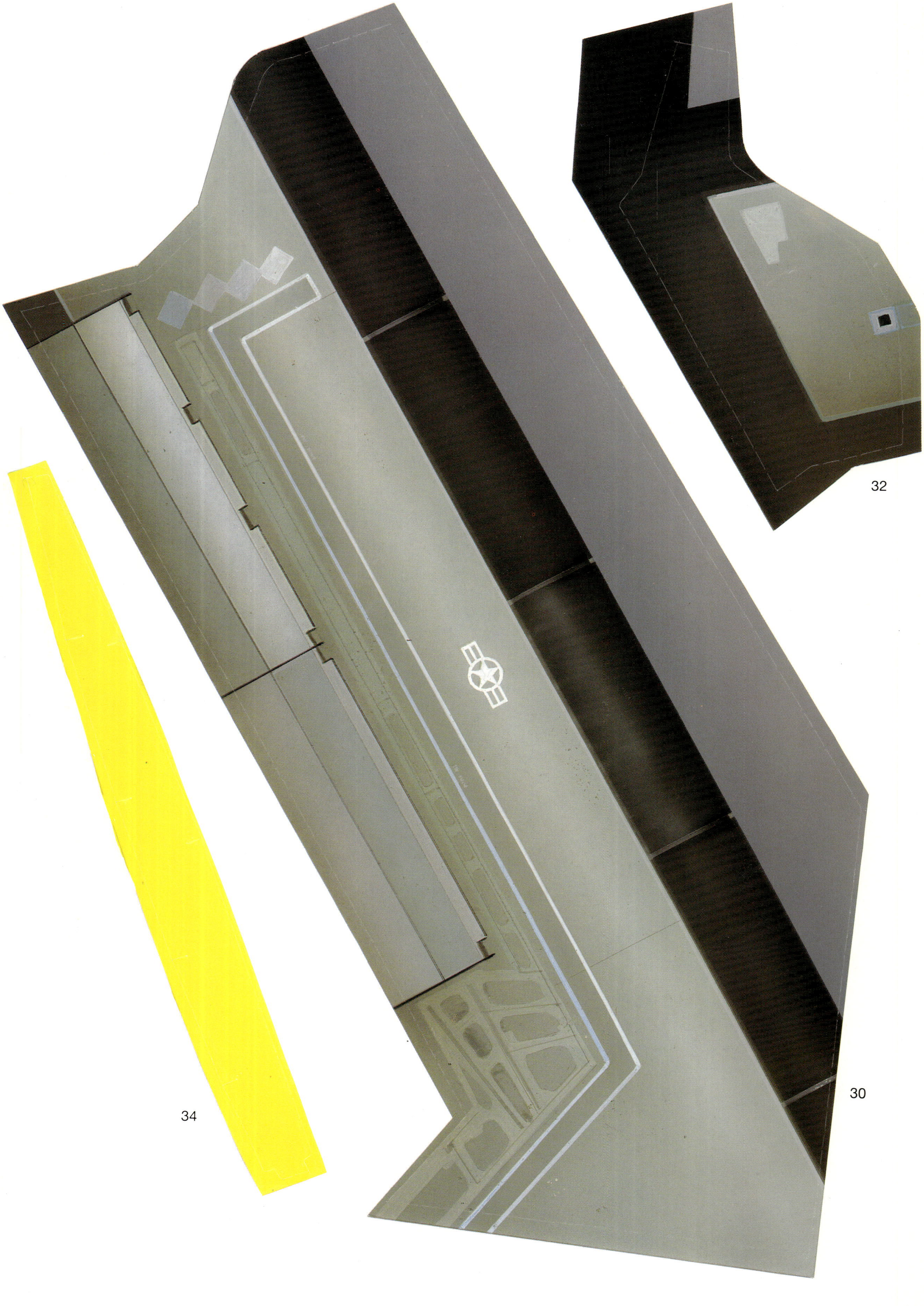

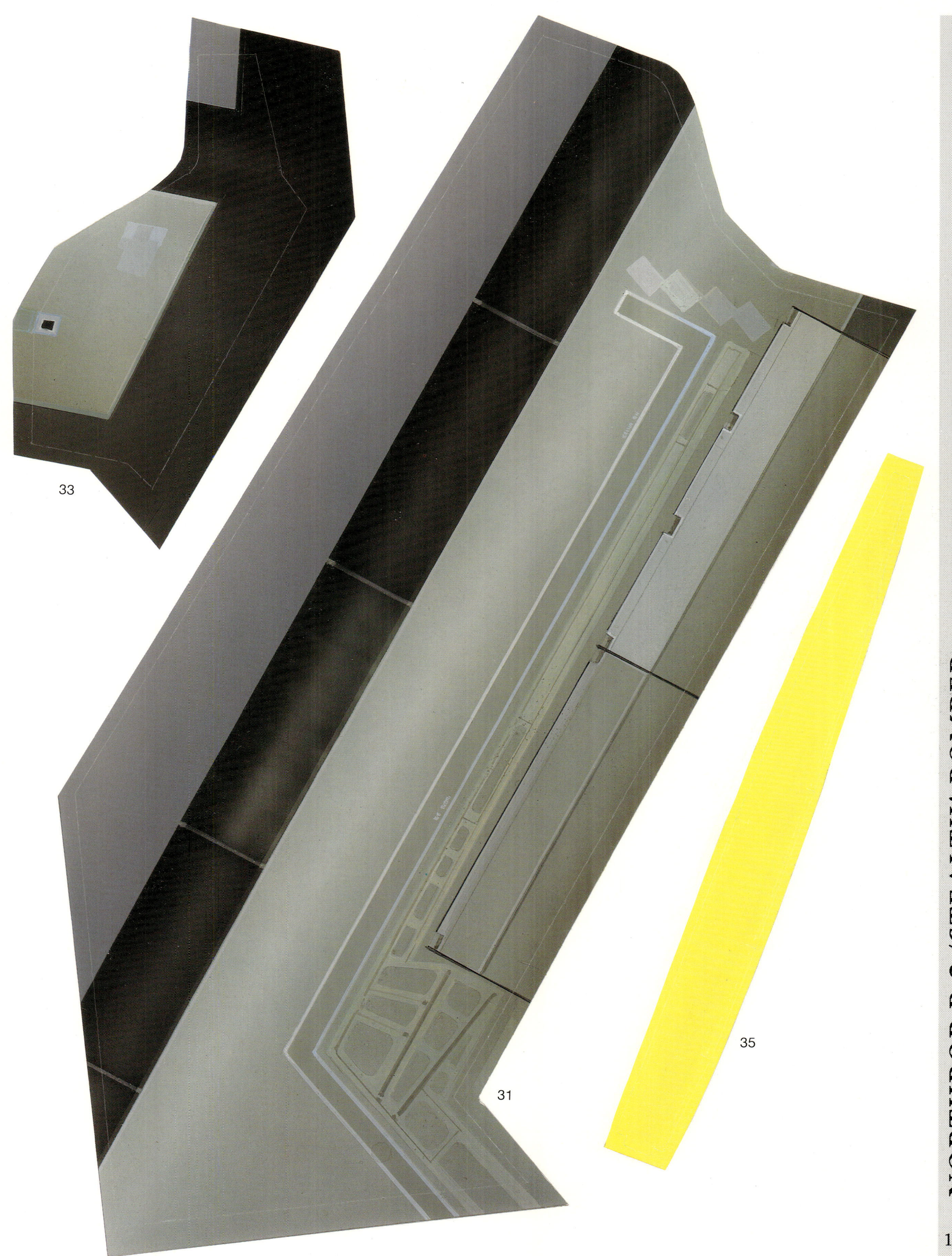

33
31
35

44
41
45